CAROLINE PRINCESS OF WALES
& OTHER FORGOTTEN PEOPLE OF HISTORY

National Portrait Gallery, London

By Keith R. Dawson

Eloquent Books

Eloquent Books
An imprint of Strategic Book Group
P.O. Box 333
Durham CT 06422
www.StrategicBookGroup.com

ISBN 978-1-60911-690-3

Printed in the United States of America

Caroline Princess of Wales

\+

Samuel Enderby IV

\=

William Enderby
An unknown story based on facts

DEDICATION

To the staff of Toowoomba Library and the National Archives, London, To my Doctor Peter Beeston and numerous other doctors who have kept me alive for the last twenty odd years whilst I have been writing and researching this book.

TABLE OF CONTENTS

SWEET CAROLINE

Caroline Amelia Elizabeth of Brunswick was glad that the break with George had been made; it had been coming from the first night when he lay drunk in the fireplace. She had to force herself onto a partially disrobed George, after he had relieved himself. Getting him onto the ottoman had been a strenuous task; thank goodness they were both fertile and she had become pregnant in that one occasion. Hand work had to be employed to get him ready—thanks to the stable boy in Brunswick who showed her how to do it.

It would have been nice to have brought Charlotte with her but that was too much to ask. At least she would be able to see her, as her new home—the vicarage at Charlton to which she was going—was not too far from London. It was a bit out of the way in the country, far enough for George not to bother her.

First impressions are important and the first impression of the vicarage was all bad. It was dark, dingy, dilapidated, with awful furniture, shutters not curtains; everything was dark brown in colour. Even the servants were of a gloomy appearance, which was not surprising if they had to work in this house. Things will have to be changed one way or another; she would have to ask Hester what could be done. Caroline would long remember that first night: strange shadows, the house creaking and groaning in the wind. Caroline went to sleep that night with the cheerful thought that at least the wind was coming from Brunswick where her father would be thinking of her.

Next morning, Caroline sent a note to the Stanhopes to see if Hester could come to the Vicarage. The footman came back with the unpleasant news that Hester was in London with her uncle, "Pitt the Younger," the Prime Minister of Britain, and not expected to return for at least a week. After breakfast, Caroline went for a walk in the extensive gardens almost as unimaginative as the house: just grass, orchard, and vegetable plot that contained nothing. At least there would be apples. Picking one that looked ripe from the tree, Caroline suddenly thought of Eve; there was no grub in the apple, that had been left behind and no Adam in sight. Returning to the house, Caroline decided to explore the village of Charlton. The coachman, in his tactful way, suggested that the horses should be rested after the long haul of yesterday with two ladened coaches, and it was not the first time that week the horses had done the journey. Horses were Caroline's favourite animal. She loved to go riding, astride the animals back; the thought of that reminded her of her wedding night. At least now she would be able to go riding again.

Caroline walked to the church accompanied by a maid and a footman who told her that this part of England was noted for its Protestant religion before and after King Henry the Eighth in his palace at nearby Greenwich had created the Church of England. They walked into the village scandalising the inhabitants who recognised her, that a princess would walk around the village. Caroline could see the consternation in their looks at her; well, she thought, they had better get used to it. The village was rural in outlook and situation but the walk had done her good. She was ready for lunch.

The house was getting on everybody's nerves and they had been there only two days. No one had any person of their standing to speak with and Caroline mused that females appear to need to talk far more than most men. She realised that she had this need for society and did not think she could be a farmer's wife. The isolation was not good. There were no children to see or hear, certainly none to look after or to give a cuddle to. Being aware that females talk could also be used to advantage. Caroline let it be known to her staff that she was dissatisfied with the house and was willing to move.

Next day, with the horses rested and Caroline suspected the coachman also, she went for a tour of exploration of the neighbourhood. Charlton was separated from its neighbours by agricultural fields and a forest of beech and oak trees. A lot of the roads were tracks made by constant use therefore completely without any road building material. The ruts made the journey interesting; you knew somebody of importance lived nearby because of the improvement in the road surface. Coming through the forest to Shooters Hill, she had the coachman turn right to take them to the top of Crooms Hill in the area of Earl of Chesterfield's House and other houses just before the hill went down to Greenwich passing the church of St. Alphege, one of the first English Christian martyrs. The coach had come up Crooms hill on its way to Charlton, but having faced the horses, she had not seen the vista and was unprepared for the expansive view of London from the top of Crooms Hill. St. Paul's Cathedral stood out majestically on its rise, above the palace of Westminster and surprisingly above the Tower of London. The majestic Thames River could be seen winding its way past the new docks being constructed downstream of the obstructive but necessary bridges. No wonder the Earl of Chesterfield had built his house on the hill top.

Caroline wondered whose houses were on the opposite side of the road. The first one was attractive, especially with the circular tower. The whole building looked as if it had been a windmill and the miller's house; it was larger than the Vicarage and built out of brick. On second thought, the place had an air of neglect as if no one cared for it. Come to think about it, there was no sign of activity by any person, cat or dog. The grounds were well treed but kept away from the house. Caroline had the coachman halt the horses. When he did, she could hear the sounds of children. Determined to find out about the house, she had the coachman drive up the next drive. As he did so, the sound of children was louder, some of whom ran inside at the coach's approach to tell the adults that visitors had arrived. By the time Caroline had alighted from her coach, a woman about her own age was approaching her. Both women eyeing each other up and liking what they saw, made for a convivial meeting, which soon took place in the lounge room over cups of Chinese tea.

The woman's name was Mary Enderby, wife of Samuel Enderby, oil merchants and ship owners. The children making the noise were George, age three and Elizabeth, age five.

Samuel, age eight was away at school. As there was more noise than two voices could make, Caroline assumed that there were children from the orphanage next door, run by Mary's sister Elizabeth and brother-in-law, Charles Enderby. Over a second cup of tea, Caroline broached the subject of the house next door, which Mary told her was empty and in the control of the Duke of Buccleuch. It had been the home of the Earl of Sandwich who had died in recent times after a tragic life that he tried to forget by being at the card table with Caroline's husband. The family name of the Earl was Montagu with no *e* on the end; hence the house name was Montagu House Cooms Hill, not to be confused with Montague House a short distance away, the house of the Dukes of Manchester.

The Earl of Sandwich, after whom people were beginning to call meat between two pieces of bread a sandwich, had married a Lady Fane who had been of unsound mind after the birth of a son and heir. She lived with her sister Elizabeth in an apartment in Windsor Castle and had been declared "De Lunatico Inquirendo" in May 1767. The Earl, at age eleven, had inherited the title from his grandfather after his father had been burnt to death at sea.

The Earl and the Enderbys had a love for music, the Earl having regular musical evenings at his house. Having separated from his wife but not divorced, he took a young opera singer as a mistress by the name of Martha Ray. During the twenty-year liaison, Martha was to bear the Earl five children, all of whom bore the name Montagu.

A shopkeeper/soldier/priest named James Hackman had been invited to a musical evening where he met and formed an infatuation for Martha Ray, ten years his senior. With no evidence of any reciprocation, he accosted her on the steps of Covent Garden as she was getting in her coach, pulling at her clothes; she fell to the ground. Hackman had two pistols. With one he killed Ray; the other he used on himself. Not making a success of it, he was tried and hanged.

In spite of its history, Caroline thought the house was far superior to the Vicarage and she liked this young woman with children, who told Caroline before she left that she was pregnant and should give birth the following year but to keep quiet about it as her husband did not know. Caroline felt honoured that she should be told and it proved that there was a bond of friendship to be had, something she had not had since leaving Brunswick. Really, the two of them had been like a house on fire and so thought her maid and the coachman, who were hospitably treated by the house staff.

The journey home was done at a smart pace so that Caroline could compose a letter to the Duke of Buccleuch. The letter was written and delivered the following day, the footman returning with a note that the Duchess would be pleased to lease the house to Caroline but things had to be done legally, which may take a few weeks.

Caroline celebrated Christmas in her new home in the traditional German way, with the absence of snow, which Caroline liked in small doses so she did not pine too much, except for her daughter, Charlotte. Hester Stanhope spent most of her Christmas with Caroline, her father not in a celebratory mood. They planned to go for a holiday together in the spring to Cornwall; Hester was to arrange the accommodation with the Elliots of Mount Edgecombe, St. Germains, near Saltash, who were related to the Pitts/Stanhopes through marriage. Lord Elliot was in partnership with Samuel Enderby II in land development. Christmas over, Caroline spent time at the Enderby orphanage lending a hand by playing with the younger ones, the need for her daughter being quietened by the contact.

During the Easter Parliamentary recess, she went with Hester to Cornwall, a long journey taking nearly a week, sometimes staying at or really taking over a coaching house, which suddenly seemed to have more than the usual number of customers who came to see her. This was a new experience for Caroline. It did not become a nuisance as on other nights, her retinue was accommodated at various noblemen's residences.

Caroline enjoyed the southeastern corner of Cornwall; the Edgecombe gardens were a spring garden as were the hedgerows. The Cornish hedges were hardly hedges but rock walls filled with earth so that they looked like a green bank but in spring they were covered with primroses in abundance. The Cornish hedge provided cover against the westerly winds, making nice picnic spots. One day, with the wind blowing from the southwest, they all went down the River Lyhner in the Edgecombe's yacht to Trematon Castle near Saltash; this was the castle of the monarch that Francis Drake had placed his Spanish loot in whilst he went to report to Queen Elizabeth I and to be knighted. Caroline got the giggles when walking up the very steep road from the creek to the castle. She kept thinking of the men walking up this steep incline with gold and diamonds on their backs; any minute, she expected to see a gold chalice, ruby encrusted, come rolling down the hill. She wondered if she would find a ruby or an emerald in the roadside if she looked.

Upon returning to Montagu House, she was informed that there was a new arrival next door. She immediately went to visit the mother and Charles Enderby and found all was well. If she could only have had her daughter with her, life would have been pleasant. Weekly visits were not the best, nor were they designed to be by that bastard of a husband; a good job the father-in-law had laid the law down else she would not be allowed the weekly visit. Caroline, because of her free and easy manner with everyone, was well liked by most who knew her. She was different in temperament and outlook from most of the Nobility. With the help of Hester, when not required by her uncle the Prime Minister, Caroline had musical evenings, carrying on the Montagu tradition with a similar result eventually. Hester was largely responsible for the guest lists initially, she being in the know as to who was in town, available and suitable for attendance. After a while, Caroline knew a circle of people she invited. Caroline's parties began to be talked about mainly because of her behaviour being considered by the times to be unladylike. Her lifestyle, she had decided, was to be the same as for the male. She could do what her husband was doing; what was good for the gander was good for the goose. This attitude led to the opinion that Caroline was at the forefront in the emancipation of women, who were not considered by society or the law to be a man's equal.

The one person she felt she could really trust was Mary

Enderby, who she visited in Mary's quiet time in the afternoon when the children were in the nursery having a sleep. A son, Henry, was born in 1800; daughter Mary was born in 1802. There seemed to be always a baby in a cot, which Caroline envied. Mary was pregnant again, near to her time. Caroline was sure of Mary's true friendship when Mary told Caroline that the newly born daughter was to be christened Caroline Enderby, which, by Mary's age of thirty-seven, could be the last child.

The friendship was a mutual admiration society: Caroline admired Mary for her children and a full life; Mary for Caroline by the way that she was speaking up for herself against the generally accepted. Caroline was gaining the respect of a lot of females who were beginning to think for themselves although still tied to the family by financial strings; some things were gaining acceptance, such as a woman being allowed to look after her own financial affairs. The lease on Montagu House was negotiated by the king's officials with the Duchess of Buccleuch, not the Duke.

One female companion, Lady Douglas, Caroline suspected of using their friendship to further her husband's army career, so Caroline decided to pay her back. This she did by spreading anonymous letters that Lady Douglas was telling tales that Caroline was pregnant. These tales were started by Caroline, by quite deliberately telling her coffee lounge maid that she was in the "family way" knowing full well that Lady Douglas was in the habit of going to the coffee room for a morning cup and that because of a female's need to talk, she would eventually get told of the pregnancy. In due course, Lady Douglas was told and she confided in her husband. The pair decided to await events for an opportune time to use the information. Because Caroline was plump and the clothes fashion not being tight fitting, it was easy to disguise a pregnancy.

Time went on and nothing happened. Caroline decided to give the accounts a push along by adopting a son of a local worker who was having a difficult time. The ruse worked to the extent that general gossip took up the story. Then, Sir John Douglas went to the brothers of Caroline's husband, the Prince of Wales, with his tale, his wife receiving a life pension of £200. Eventually there was an enquiry into Caroline's conduct; the Secretary of the enquiry was an American Loyalist by the name of George Chalmers, who was known to Samuel Enderby. The enquiry took just six weeks to exonerate her: *that in the year 1802 she was not delivered of any child, nor has anything appeared to us which would warrant the belief that she was pregnant in that year or at any other period within the compass of our enquiries— 14 July 1806.*

It was fortunate that the enquiry was for the time she adopted William Austin; if it had been two years later, things may have been different.

Mary Enderby, helped by her sister Elizabeth, from next door, put on a Sunday dinner fit for a king, to which any captain of an Enderby ship in port was invited along as a matter of course together with a suitable companion. If Caroline was not entertaining, she had a standing invitation to attend. She liked these dinners, especially when a sea captain turned up and found himself sitting next to the Princess of Wales, who inevitably thawed the old sea dog out. Then there were people like the Enderbys' friend Gov. King from New South Wales with his Devonian wife. Children were accommodated for Sunday dinner at the Enderby orphanage next door until the day they were able to attend the family occasion.

It was one such Sunday that Caroline really met the son, Samuel. She had seen him, of course, when he came home from school but the period between 5 years and 16 years did not really interest Caroline, not being academic; learning, except by contact with people, did not interest her. One Sunday dinner at the Enderby's, the talk was all about the French Emperor Napoleon and the imminence of an invasion of England, which of course was of great interest to shipping people and the inhabitants of the south of England. To change the subject, Caroline brought up the subject of scarcity of labour due to Napoleon, that she wanted a hole dug to make a Roman type Bath and could not get anybody suitable to dig it. Samuel's ears pricked up like a beagle. He was at a loose end: home from school for the summer holidays, with another year to go at school, he was not allowed in the family firms premises at Paul's Wharfe in the city. His father and uncles were too busy working to teach him anything of the oil trade and shipping to St. Petersburg. Things would change next year but in the meantime, he had to find something to do. So on the Monday following, he went next door to offer his services in digging the excavation for the Roman Bath.

Samuel was known to the Princess's staff, so when he asked to see the Princess, he was shown to her presence in her boudoir, where she was finishing getting ready for the day. No one thought it odd; he was the boy from next door whom she had known for five or six years. Caroline had forgotten momentarily what she had learnt in the stables in Brunswick at his age. It was the first time Samuel had become aware of the cleavage of a woman's breast; it made him splutter his thoughts on the Roman Bath. With a smile, Caroline put him at his ease and he repeated his thought that he could and would be pleased to have something worthwhile to do during the summer holidays, so could he dig the excavation for the bath? Caroline had another look at Samuel and found that he was no longer a schoolboy but nearly a man. He was not far from being six feet tall and a broad shoulder to go with it. She thought he would be able to do the job and told him to start when he liked.

Samuel was pleased to have something to do. Most of the morning he spent in acquiring a shovel, a long-handled shovel, a pick, a crowbar and a wheelbarrow from various gardeners who were pleased to see one of the young masters willing to do some manual work. They gave him advice as what to expect when he got below the soil. They pointed out to him that he would soon be digging the underlying chalk, which once you got a start, it was not too hard, but slow going. The family's gardener said he should have a look at the Blackheath Caverns that had been dug many decades ago. By the time he had assembled his tools, he thought it was too late to start. Then he realised he did not know where to start or what size and shape.

Next day, a little later than the previous day, he called on the Princess to ascertain where and what he was to dig. After a short wait, Caroline went out into the treed garden with him to show him where she wanted the Roman Bath. Caroline had

put a lot of thought into the siting of the bath; she led him to
a spot that could not be seen because of trees, except for the
way they had come. The bath had to be rectangular with steps
down the way they had come and that he had to allow for the
thickness of the walls, other than that he could make it whatever size he found easy to dig. By eleven o'clock the next day,
Samuel had removed all the grass and soil to expose the white
chalk when Caroline came to inspect what had been done.

Samuel told Caroline about the Blackheath Caverns, which
was news to her. The antiquity and mystery of who had
excavated them interested Caroline, so it came about that
Samuel and Caroline with servants arranged to go and inspect
the caverns. Their idea proved popular. Soon there was a large
contingent of Enderbys, Hester Stanhope, her father, to
everyone's surprise, plus members of Caroline's household.
Caroline thought how her daughter, Charlotte, would have
liked to have been there, but alas, the Prince of Wales would
not allow it. The caverns were deep and high to the curved
ceiling. The who and why of the digging baffled them all—it
seemed that work had been curtailed before finishing. The size
of the excavation showed Samuel that the digging could not
have been hard going. The next day proved the point: it was
messy when wet, the chalk sticking to the shovel, and the wet
chalk proving heavy in the wheelbarrow.

Samuel was down below waist height in the chalk when
Caroline came to inspect the progress. Looking down at his
muscular back, glistening with perspiration from his exertions,
she realised that he was almost a man. Her memory shot back
to the stable boy in Brunswick and that moment when she

knew she had become a woman, in mind if not in body. Caroline stood close to where Samuel had to climb out of the excavation. He could not refrain from looking at Caroline's cleavage as he straightened up from exiting the excavation. Caroline was aware of his look and instantly clasped his face to her bosom and carried out what she had been taught in a stable when she was his age.

Caroline got into the habit of taking a light lunch for Samuel on her morning inspections. The inevitable occurred. Caroline found herself pregnant. Fortunately, the excavation was finished by this time and Samuel was soon to be on his way back to school for his final year. Caroline told him her news, which when it had sunk in, he realised he was in trouble. Then he realised they were both in trouble. He had got the Queen-of-England-to-be pregnant!

Samuel Enderby Sr. was away in the North of England on business when Samuel Jr. told his news to his mother, Mary, who was understandably shocked into silence for a few minutes. She was disappointed that a friend would allow this to happen. Then the quality that Governor King of Australia told his son Mrs. Enderby had, came to the fore. At this point, Caroline was announced. She had allowed Samuel to tell his mother, her friend, but had then come to support him and plead forgiveness for herself. Governor King had told his son that if the generals and admirals had half as much ability as Mary Enderby, the nation would not have lost America.

Mary Enderby saw the whole problem immediately and what must be done to minimise or cover up the events that would happen. Mary told Samuel Jr. that he would have to await his father's pleasure when he returned. Caroline was to gradually reduce all parties and visitors so that in three months, they would cease, and she was to wear clothing that would hide the fact of increased weight and shape. When the time came, she was to come to her where the birth would take place and she would raise the child, pointing out that she would have to take care that she did not get pregnant, and that the best way to ensure that was to abstain from intercourse, which would not go down well with her husband.

Samuel Sr. returned from his business trip full of the news that the talk in the London Coffee Houses was that the Prince of Wales was trying to get his father to have an enquiry into whether or not the Princess of Wales had had an illegitimate child in 1802 in the form of William Austin. Samuel Jr. sat through the dinner listening to this gossip hardly eating anything, contrary to his usual appetite. At the dinner's end, Mary pushed the conversation to the fact that Samuel Jr. had something to say to his father and that they had better go to his study to do it, which they did.

Mary was concerned at the silence emanating from the study, where Samuel Sr. had been shocked into silence, so that the two Samuels sat looking at each other when she entered the room. Samuel Sr., upon his wife entering the room, said that one bit of gossip he had not told them was that Hester Stanhope, niece of the Prime Minister for whom she was Housekeeper at No. 10 Downing Street, was reputed to be saying that impregnating the Queen of England was high treason, for which there was only one punishment— beheading. After letting that be absorbed, he reminded them that probably his great-great-grandfather had ended his life in such a manner when Charles II returned to the throne. Mary told her husband what she had arranged with Caroline. Samuel, upon hearing her out, was thankful that he had chosen a wife with good sense. What she proposed, if kept quiet, would be the best way out. Much as he would like to kick her backside, Caroline had better keep coming to the house so that when the time came for her confinement, spending a day or so here would not be remarkable. For the first time, he spoke to Samuel Jr. telling him just what he could expect if anything was to be said out of that room. Samuel Jr. was to make himself scarce, to lose himself amongst the military forthwith, and he was not to expect anything from him or the firm in monetary terms. He had to forego his inheritance. In September 1804, Samuel Jr. joined the Queen's Lancers.

One day in April 1805, Caroline went to her friend Mary Enderby early one morning. Fortunately, Caroline had obeyed instructions, more through not wishing to inflict publicity and legal approbation upon the family than for her own sake. Mary had been making preparations for weeks not knowing the actual date but making sure things would be ready, whenever. A bedroom had been readied with the four poster bed of King Henry VIII and his Queen Catherine of Aragon that had been in the Enderby family for centuries. So it came to pass that William Enderby was born in a royal bed of a royal mother. It was fortunate that Mary, a mother of seven children, knew what to do and that Caroline had as little difficulty as with her daughter, Charlotte. Before Samuel Sr. arrived home, all was ship shape and Bristol fashion.

Samuel Jr. had kept in touch with his mother who told him that he had a son to be named William after his Brunswick grandfather. The news made Samuel think that he did not have much to lose, so he volunteered to man the ships that were being assembled for an expected sea battle with Napoleon's navy. Because he was in the defence forces, he could get a three-year transfer to the Navy; this he did, seeing service at the battle of Trafalgar in *HMS Defence*. After writing to his mother telling her that he was assigned to *HMS Defence*, he received in an unmarked package, a handsome red silk neckerchief together with a superior needle kit. The beauty of the neckerchief caused him to receive some jocular attention from his shipmates who would wear red neckerchiefs in battle, to be used as emergency bandages and tourniquets.

Happily, his was not so used and is on display at the Greenwich Maritime Museum and on the net under Samuel Enderby.

THE FACTS

One day during World War II, when visiting Enderby grandparents in Boston, Lincolnshire, United Kingdom, Grandfather Henry Enderby received a large parcel. When unwrapped, it was a large glass case containing a model of a sailing ship. My mother told me that we were related to the Whaling Enderbys and that part of Antarctica was named after the Enderbys and that an Enderby sailed with Capt. Cook to Australia.

I now know that the model was of the ship *Samuel Enderby* which had been caused to be built by Charles II, Henry and George II, sons of Samuel Enderby III and grandsons of Samuel Enderby II, in whose memory the ship was commemorated and was a useful addition to their fleet of ships. The model had been made by the Isle of Wight Shipbuilders son and is now in the Maritime Museum in Greenwich, United Kingdom. The seeing of this model in the circumstances caused the author to research the whaling Enderbys. Charles II, Henry, and George II did not marry. Henry is reputed to have had an illegitimate child with a married woman, following in the footsteps of his older brother.

Only William had male children to carry on the Enderby name. The fact that William had nothing to do with the family firm made me curious; then when I found that he and his family lived in Scotland with no visible means of support, my curiosity increased. That Herman Melville used the ship *Samuel Enderby* in his book *Moby Dick* and had the following to say about the Enderbys increased the interest in my ancestors:

"The ship was named after the late Samuel Enderby, merchant of London, the original of the famous whaling house of Enderby and Sons, a house which in my poor whaleman's opinion, comes not far behind the united Royal houses of the Tudors and Bourbons, in point of real historical interest."

William (Enderby) is mysterious because I do not *know* who his parents were and cannot find an official account of his birth, which did not have to be registered with a government department before 1838. I believe that William is the child of **Caroline Amelia Princess of Wales and Samuel Enderby IV.** Only William had children to have descendents named Enderby. The legitimate descendents of Samuel IV are female.

The erroneously named "Nephews and Nieces Letter" amongst the General Gordon of Khartoum Papers in the British Library, indicates that this William had a son and a grandson named William, just like my grandfather Henry Enderby's father was a William as was his father and grandfather. That is why my grandfather Enderby received the model of the sailing ship *Samuel Enderby*, (see *Moby Dick* chapters *100* and *101*) in accordance with the will of Mrs. Moffit and Blunt, which stated that the model was to go to all descendents of Samuel Enderby for a period of time before it was accepted by the National Maritime Museum in Greenwich, where it now resides. So someone knew who was who.

Mrs. Moffitt was Samuel Enderby III's granddaughter and younger sister of General Gordon of Khartoum. She was Helen Clarke Gordon who married Chinese Gordon's medical colleague of the Chinese Opium Wars, Dr. Moffit. Helen's middle name Clarke is a pointer to another historic fact of another story.

The "Nephews and Nieces Letter" states that William Enderby, born about 1805, married Mary Howis/Howe/Howl. The letter does not state when he died, so presumably he was still alive at the time of writing which was 1875. Why is William mentioned in this letter but not any of the other eight children of Samuel III and Mary Goodwyn? This letter, misnamed by historians, tells of a lot of the Enderby doings. It is unaddressed and unsigned. It was amongst the Moffit/Blunt papers accepted by the British Library. A phrase in Mrs. Moffit's will is very similar to one in the letter. This, plus where the letter came from, is the reason I maintain it was in all probability written by Mrs. Moffit. Colonel Moffit, her son, also has an informative letter in the collection. This letter mentions the Henry VIII bed, and that he slept in it when a little boy, insisting on sleeping below Henry's Coat of Arms, not Catherine's. He is also the informant that Amelia Enderby, known to the younger members of the family as Aunt Amy, was a dwarf. When I read that it reminded me that my mother told me that my grandfather Enderby had a dwarf aunt.

William is mentioned in a letter by C. Macarthur (nephew of Australia's infamous John MacArthur) to Captain Phillip Parker King RN, (son of Australian Governor King,) dated August 22 1826, *"in that he had seen a good deal of William*

Enderby, he had gone up to Blackheath with him and the two of them had been to weddings," this confirms that 1805 could be William's birth year as in the anonymous letter.

C. MacArthur (1792-1827) is related to Hannibal Hawkins MacArthur. He dies young, not long after the letter was written. Marnie Bassett, in the book *The Henty's* says the *C* is for Charles, a lieutenant in the Royal Navy, a nephew of John MacArthur and son of James MacArthur and Catherine Hannibal Hawkins. C. MacArthur may have known William because of Hannibal Hawkins MacArthur marrying Anna Maria King, who was largely raised by Charles Enderby and wife Elizabeth nee Goodwyn at 66/64 Coombes Hill, where the orphanage was. Elizabeth leaves most of her estate to niece Catherine Hawkins.

* * *

A letter to P.P. King upon his return to London in 1830 from surveying Cape Horn by recently widowed Mrs. Mary Enderby, (SAM III) is as follows:

29 Oct. 1830

I most sincerely congratulate you on your safe return to England, and trust that it will not be many days before we see you here and I can assure you that it will give me very great pleasure to see Phillip. I can at present accommodate him with a small bed that his brother used to sleep in and if you are at liberty to accept it, Charle's bed is at your service for the next fortnight as he is going, partly on pleasure and partly on business to the North. George has your letter for the information contained in there he is much obliged.__ There are plenty of Flys at Woolwich, and our dinner hour is Saturday, Sunday and Monday at five—Tuesday Wednesday Thursday and Friday at six. As we never dine out you will be sure to find some of the family; this day Major Gordon dines here in consequence of Elizabeth having a Ball and supper, the party consists of about ninety. Therefore he cannot find room to eat in his own house. If Mr. Jones is the hearing of this, he will tell you that Caroline intends to join the Festive party in the evening and will take up as much room as half a dozen single Ladies. Williams's wife is very unwell in consequence of a fright, for forty-eight hours scarcely expected to live and she is at present so that she is on the Sofa. Mrs. Enderby is expected home this month She set out on her travels with young — and his sister, but they separated after quitting B—, the girl returned home and Mrs. E. wants the remainder of her tour alone, but Mr. Don S— this will give you the best account. A letter from Sam about this week past, mentions that he proposes getting leave of absence this month to return to England, it was very short, in it he said a long one —in reading to be sent, but it has not come to hand. The sooner I see you and your son the more pleasure it will give dear Captain King.

Yours very sincerely, Mary Enderby.

William Enderby and Mary Howe[?] married between the letter dates of 22 August 1826 and 29 October 1830. Sam III's will, dated 1829, shows William as unmarried.

The Capt. King would be Phillip Parker King RN., later Admiral King and Commissioner in Australia for the Australian Agricultural Company. Flys in this context is a carriage for hire.

Mrs. Enderby may be Mrs. George Enderby, nee Henrietta Samson—she had also been widowed in 1829, and had apparently gone on holiday—or the writer's sister Elizabeth Goodwyn, widow of Charles Enderby I, who died in 1819. The Sam mentioned would be Sam IV, he was in the army in India, age 41 years. Mary Enderby in 1830 can only be Mary Goodwyn, wife of Samuel III. The fact that William's wife was on the sofa also suggests Mrs. Sam III. Charle's bed can only be referring to Charles Enderby II (1798-1876), the one who was due to lose the family's money in the Auckland Isles twenty years later. George is George Enderby II, Sam IV's brother. In 1830, Phillip, the son of P.P. King, would be 13.

The remark about Caroline's size may be alluding to a pregnancy, nine months since marriage to Naval Lieut. William Dow.

* * *

The originals of these letters are in the British Library, London. The Mitchell Library in Sydney has copies, as I have. The original letters are in the Blunt collection; Helen [Mrs. Moffit] was the family squirrel or historian. When she died, Mrs Gerald Blunt, a sister, inherited them. Because the papers contained a lot of information about General Gordon of Khartoum, the British Library accepted the papers, which also contained Enderby papers largely ignored by historians except for the so-called *Nephew and Nieces Letter.*

Nephew William is left money in wills of the Enderby family. *In three different letters and at least three wills, William is shown to exist by differing people.* In the wills, William is always referred to as Nephew William never as William Enderby.

Samuel Enderby III, in his last will and testament of 1829, claims William as his son, but William, the youngest, and Samuel IV, the eldest, are treated differently from the other three sons, Charles II, Henry and George II; neither Samuel IV or William has anything to do with the family firm, and both are left less money, which is for their wives and children, not themselves.

Samuel Enderby III lived at Loretta House, 68 Crooms Hill, Blackheath, which is today the Presbytery for the Catholic Church next door, which was built in the garden of No. 68. The Fourth Earl of Sandwich, he who the bread snack is named for, lived in Montagu House, Crooms Hill, Blackheath, Sam's near neighbour on the south side.

Caroline of Brunswick married her cousin George, Prince of Wales, to produce an heir to the English throne; nine months after the marriage with the drunken Prince, who is reported to have spent his wedding night in the fire grate, Princess Caroline gave birth to a daughter, to be named Charlotte after her Grandmother, the Queen of King George III. The Royal couple separated within a year. Carlton House not being large enough to separate the two, King George III, who liked Caroline, arranged for her to occupy Charlton Vicarage and when found not to be to Caroline's liking he established her in Montagu House, Blackheath, near Greenwich. Some sources say the house was leased from the

Duchess of Buccleuch, but this does not explain how George IV could demolish the house in 1815, when Caroline Amelia, Princess of Wales, went to the Continent on an extended holiday. Some people say Caroline lived in Shrewsbury House, Shooters Hill, some say that the Pagoda belonging to the Duke of Dartmouth was also a garden house for Caroline. I suspect historians are getting the Montagu(e) Houses mixed up. The Montagues, family name of the Dukes of Manchester, had a Montague House not far away in Blackheath. To distinguish between the two separate families, it is important to spell the names correctly.

In the City of London Collage collection of paintings Montagu House is not clearly defined. J. Baker's painting of Montagu House is not strictly correct—the house with a round tower is further away from the two white buildings according to the 1794 map of the Blackheath Hundred and has a road between. I believe both houses were part of Caroline's establishment, the round mill tower being the room contemporary writing refers to as a circular room for dancing, the Old Mill being used for entertainment nights. Where these three houses were is still open ground today. Ground that was owned by the king?

Samuel Enderby III, and his father before him, had been the whaling industry's CEO/spokesperson, to the governments of the day, also on transatlantic shipping. Two of the three Boston Tea Party ships, the party which initiated the American War of Independence, and the colonising of Australia, were Enderby ships, one carrying Sam II's daughter Mary on her honeymoon. Charles 1 and Samuel III buying sister Mary a book of bound musical manuscripts by Dr's Arne and Burney, which included Rule Britannia, for a wedding present, and is now in the Glasgow University Library, suggests the family had an interest in music as did the Earl of Sandwich.

Charles Enderby and wife, Elizabeth Goodwyn, lived at 66/64 Crooms Hill, Blackheath. One number was their residence, the other their orphanage that this childless couple ran, and where the formative years of Anna Maria King [Australian Gov. King's daughter, sister of Admiral P.P. King,] were spent before she married Hannibal Hawkins MacArthur and moved to Australia to live, and is buried at Ipswich, Queensland. Charles was an executor for her till she was twenty-one years of age.

Widowed Emelia Vansittart and seven children lived at 60 Crooms Hill, Blackheath. Emelia, widow of the Superintendent of the East India Company lost at sea in 1770, was a long time investor in Enderby ships. The brand new ship to be the first whaler officially around Cape Horn in 1788 is named after her, Emelia, not Amelia as is often incorrectly stated. Of her five sons, one became an Admiral, another a General and Nicholas the British treasurer under various governments for twelve years. A daughter had a Blue School which is remembered in an Enderby Will.

Princess of Wales, Caroline Amelia Elizabeth of Brunswick-Wolfenbuttel (1768-1821), Queen of the United Kingdom of Great Britain and Ireland, consort of King George IV, was born on 17 May 1768 to Princess Augusta, sister of King George III of the United Kingdom. Caroline was brought up in the informal atmosphere of the ducal court, which did not have a pretence at sophistication, and her father having a reputation for the ladies. At fourteen, she was described as a lively, pretty child with light-coloured hair hanging in curls on her neck, with rosebud lips. She remained extrovert and frivolous in her manner, but was kind-hearted, good-natured, fond of children, and enjoyed society. Caroline was chosen as the intended bride of her cousin George, Prince of Wales [George IV of Great Britain] partly because her mother was a favourite sister of George III, and the favourable reports of her given by the Prince's brothers, the Dukes of York and Clarence, when they visited Germany, also a lack of a suitable alternative. King George III hoped that "domestic felicity" would settle the prince's life and take his mind off a military command against the French.

The Prince of Wales had an affair with twenty-two-year-old actress, Mary Robinson, when he was seventeen years old and had secretly married Catholic widow Maria Fitzherbert in 1785. He was forced by his enormous debts [over £600,000; if Mrs. James Cook's fortune of £60,000 is equivalent to more than 20 million pounds today, the Prince's debt is at least 200 million of today's money] to seek his father's financial assistance in 1794 and it was made a condition of his relief that he should marry legitimately, to produce an heir to the throne. He was willing to desert Mrs Fitzherbert, being currently involved with Lady Jersey, but he declared that he had no interest in the choice of a bride. Lord Malmesbury, a friend of the prince, brought Caroline from Brunswick. The marriage took place on 8 April 1795 in the Chapel Royal, St James's. The prince was reportedly the worse for alcohol and had to be supported to go through the ceremony. He demanded that she should submit to his authority, which she refused to do. The only child of this stormy marriage, Princess Charlotte Augusta (1796-1817), was born on 7 January 1796; one cannot get much closer to nine months than that.

Three days after his wife's confinement, the prince wrote a will in which he declared that Mrs Fitzherbert was his only true wife, and that "to her who is call'd the Princess of Wales" he left one shilling (Correspondence of George, Prince of Wales, 3.132-40). Caroline had attempted to live on amicable terms with him, but he neglected her and she became increasingly lonely, bored, and resentful. The inevitable separation took place in 1796, despite the efforts of King George III to mediate. Caroline left Carlton House in 1797 and went to live in The Old Rectory, Charlton, [near Greenwich] moving to the Earl of Sandwich's, Montagu House, Crooms Hill, Blackheath.

King George III was fond of the new confectionary, chocolate, which he bought from the Chocolate House, 6 West Grove, Blackheath. Then he visited his daughter-in-law where, no doubt, both enjoyed his purchases. The Prince of Wales would have forbidden the Princess of Wales access to her child, but the king, who always favoured Caroline, insisted that she should be allowed to visit Charlotte.

Caroline, Princess of Wales, made no attempt to exploit her situation politically. She remained prominent in society and entertained frequently at Blackheath, often in an informal and high-spirited atmosphere. Her guests included the leading political men of the day from both parties, such as Pitt, Eldon,

Charles Grey, Prime Minister to be the assassinated Spencer Perceval, and Sir Thomas Lawrence and George Canning, with both of whom she was believed to have had affairs.

Lady Hester Stanhope, daughter of the Earl of Stanhope, was a frequent visitor and friend, accompanying the Princess of Wales on holiday in Devon and Cornwall. Lady Hester acted as housekeeper for her bachelor uncle, "Pitt the Younger" at 10 Downing Street, when he was Prime Minister, up to his death in 1806, after this Lady Hester went to Syria, to that part that is now known as Lebanon, where she became an offbeat religious leader. One story of her death is by her bricking herself up in a crypt.

Lady Douglas—with whom Princess Caroline became friendly until they quarrelled in 1803, when Lady Douglas was accused, in anonymous letters, of spreading malicious gossip about Caroline's morals, including allegations that she had borne a child since her separation from the Prince of Wales— later affirmed, that in 1802 the Princess of Wales had told her that she was *in the family way*. Sir John Douglas heard of the pregnancy from his wife in 1804; he went to the Prince's brothers telling tales to ingratiate himself. The Princess was not pregnant, although suspicions were aroused by her habit of adopting stray children, one of whom, William Austin, the son of Samuel and Sophia Austin, a Deptford shipwright, was reputed to be her natural child. Lady Douglas received a £200 pension for life from the Prince of Wales.

These unsavoury rumours led to the setting up in 1806 of an official Privy Council commission of inquiry known as the "delicate investigation," at which a Montagu House footman,

Samuel Roberts, said that "The Princess is very fond of fucking." The Princess's doctors, Mills and Edmades, both denied having told Jenny Lloyd, Caroline's Coffee room servant, that the Princess of Wales was pregnant.

The Lords Commissioners had their instructions from King George III on 29 May 1806; they concluded on 14 July 1806 that:

There is no foundation for believing that the child now with the Princess is the child of her Royal Highness, or that she was delivered of any child in the year 1802; nor has anything appeared to us which would warrant the belief that she was pregnant in that year, or at any other period within the compass of our enquiries-14 July 1806.

Does the last sentence suggest there might be something outside the compass of enquiries?

The chief clerk to the Privy Council was George Chalmers, a Loyalist American by birth, a Philadelphia lawyer and known to Samuel Enderby III. There is a letter from Samuel to Chalmers still in existence. The report found that the rumours about a pregnancy were false, but censured Caroline's "levity of conduct." King George III demanded the cabinet's advice; it recommended that he should warn the Princess about her future conduct, but, to the prince's fury, advised that she should not be excluded from the court. Caroline, Princess of Wales, continued to enjoy the king's support, but not that of the queen, who had taken a dislike to her from the outset.

Caroline's position became weaker at the king's relapse into insanity in 1810. The Prince of Wales acting as Regent, due to the king's insanity, decreed that Caroline, Princess of Wales, was to be excluded from the court and only with difficulty could she obtain permission to see her daughter, Princess Charlotte, who was educated under the Prince of Wales's supervision. Charlotte, however, resented this treatment of her mother and when in 1813 [age 16] her father demanded that she should live at Carlton House, she fled to join the Princess of Wales. A crisis was averted when Lord Grey, leader of the parliamentary opposition, refused to become embroiled in the affair and Henry Brougham, who had become adviser to both Caroline and Charlotte, persuaded the latter to submit to the Prince's paternal authority. Caroline thereupon decided to leave England and set off on a series of travels on August 14 1814, initially to Brunswick but shortly afterwards around the Mediterranean. Before leaving, she corresponded with Lord Liverpool [July 25th 1814] in which she left Montagu House, Blackheath, to Princess Charlotte, also the title of Ranger of Greenwich Park [a paid position] together with the house left to Caroline by her mother.

It is said that Caroline had been intending to travel since 1806. Caroline left Lancing, Sussex aboard frigate HMS Janson, Captain King, on 9 August 1814. She went at first with English companions but when, for various reasons, these friends returned home, she replaced them with mainly Italian followers of lower social status and reputation. Chief among them was Bartolomeo Bergami, or Pergami, a pretended Milanese baron, a man about thirty years old, tall, handsome, and of superb physique. He became successively her courier, bodyguard, groom of the bedchamber, and major-domo. *Most of 1815 was spent around Lake Como.*

Caroline's movements throughout her travels were closely

watched by paid spies, notably one Baron Ompteda who was recruited by the Regent's Hanoverian minister, Count Munster, to gather evidence against her. Almost weekly reports came in of indiscreet and scandalous behaviour, improper entertainments in which she took part, and above all of suspected intimacy with Bergami. He was alleged to have slept in communicating rooms or even in the same bed, to have shared a bed with her on board a sailing vessel in the Bay of Naples, and to have been present when she bathed. Caroline seemed to have become infatuated and to be completely under his influence. She procured for him a Sicilian barony and a knighthood of Malta and instituted for him her own order of St Caroline. His sister, Countess Oldi, became a close companion and lady of honour and two of his brothers were also taken into her service.

In 1816, legal advisers had warned the Prince of Wales that divorce in the ecclesiastical courts would be a lengthy and difficult process, particularly since he would be obliged to confess *his own adultery and illegal marriage to Catholic Mrs. Fitzherbert*. Moreover, the evidence against Caroline was of doubtful quality, being drawn almost entirely from foreigners and servants who might be suspected of taking bribes. In 1818, the prince therefore appointed a commission of three persons, William Cooke, a barrister, J.A. Powell, a solicitor, and Major J.H. Browne, who spoke some Italian, to go to Milan and gather further evidence. No proceedings had been begun before the death of George III in January 1820. The evidence collected by the *Milan Commission* was to form the basis of the accusations in the *queen's trial* later that year.

As soon as George IV became king, he took the first steps against the Princess of Wales, by ordering her exclusion from the prayers for the royal family in the Anglican liturgy. Incensed by this insult, Caroline set off for England to claim her position as queen. She was met at St Omer by Henry Brougham, whom she made her attorney-general, and by Lord Hutchinson, on behalf of the cabinet, who brought a proposal, reluctantly accepted by the king, to give her an annuity of £50,000 provided she would not cross the channel nor claim the title of queen. She peremptorily refused, despite Brougham's plea to her to negotiate a settlement. She was now also being advised by Matthew Wood, an alderman and former lord mayor of London, who represented a group of metropolitan radicals who wanted to use her to stir up opposition to the king and the government.

The queen's arrival became, as the government had feared, the occasion for widespread public rejoicings. She reached London on 6 June 1820 and went first to Alderman Wood's house in South Audley Street, later renting Brandenburg House at Hammersmith. Throughout the proceedings against her in the summer and autumn of 1820, she was the focus of many demonstrations, receiving over 350 addresses of support from all sections of the population, many from groups of women who saw her as a symbol of the oppression of their sex. She also had the support of The Times and many other opposition or radical newspapers. Her cause was now overtly political as the nation divided into two camps.

Caroline Amelia, Princess of Wales, Queen Consort to be of King George IV in the book "Memoirs of Queen Caroline" published in 1821: "*On the following day Saturday, July 29–In the afternoon, her majesty took an airing to Blackheath, in a private carriage.*" Who did she visit in Blackheath? Mrs. Mary Enderby/William, age 15? A private carriage would have no markings such as a coat of arms to attract attention and inform who was within the carriage.

The cabinet, spurred on by the vengeful king, unwillingly prepared a bill of pains and penalties to strip Caroline of her title, Queen, and to end her marriage by act of parliament. The bill was introduced into the House of Lords on 17 August. It was one of the most spectacular and dramatic events of the nineteenth century. Lord D'Acre presented a petition from the Queen to the assembled Peers in the House of Lords. Lord D'Acre was of the Champion family of whalers, who often assisted the Enderbys in whaling administration. On the second reading of the Bill in the House of Lords, the voting was 123 for the Bill, 95 against [218 votes]; on the third reading of the Bill, the voting was 108 for the Bill, 99 against [207 votes]. The bill was not proceeded with, in view of the diminishing vote and the mounting public support for the Princess. This was the nearest that Britain had become a Republic since Oliver Cromwell.

The queen's progresses to and from Westminster to attend the *trial*, as it became known, were attended by cheering crowds; deputations by the dozen visited Brandenburg House to present addresses, the newspapers published verbatim accounts of the Lords' proceedings, and the caricaturists on both sides had a field day. So obscene were some of the prints against the king that over £2500 was spent in buying them up and suppressing their publication. Against this proof of public support for the queen, the trial was doomed to failure.

The trial is said to be the first blow in the fight for Women's Rights. Many of the witnesses were believed to have been bribed or intimidated, and the widespread knowledge that George himself had had several mistresses added to the belief that Caroline was a victim, if not an entirely innocent one, of royal and political persecution. In the end, the prime minister, announced on 10 November that it would proceed no further.

The public verdict was in Caroline's favour as a wronged woman unjustly persecuted by a husband no better than she was. A great crowd turned out to witness her procession to a thanksgiving service organized by her supporters in St Paul's Cathedral on 29 November 1820. George IV was supported by the Privy Council who declared that a queen had no inherent right to coronation, which was at her husband's discretion. When she tried to force her way into the abbey on coronation day, 20 July 1821, she was humiliated by being refused entry. Less than a fortnight after the coronation, she was taken ill at the theatre, and after a short but painful illness she died, apparently of an intestinal obstruction, on 7 August 1821. Caroline had expressed a wish against an autopsy, so one was never done.

Queen Caroline wished to be buried beside her father [William] at Brunswick. Her funeral procession was intended to pass round to the north of the city of London to avoid public demonstrations. The cortege was intercepted by a crowd at Hyde Park Corner and forced to go through the city after a battle with the Life Guards, in which two men were killed by the soldiers. The coffin was eventually embarked from Harwich, her supporters placing on it as it left British waters the inscription *"Caroline, the injured Queen of England"* Her body was taken to Brunswick and laid in the ducal vault on 24 August. She named William Austin as her heir, but he is reported to have had a tragic life, spent several years in a lunatic asylum and died in 1846.

Caroline, Princess of Wales, craved affection, which she could not find within her own marriage, lavished it indiscreetly on others. Tied to an unwilling husband for the propagation of the royal line, the death of Princess Charlotte in 1817 made the sorry history of Caroline's marriage a farce.

[I am indebted to A.E. Smith's biography of Queen Caroline, for a lot of the non Enderby material.]

Samuel Enderby IV would have been, at least, the third generation in the business of whaling. Samuel IV was expected to carry on the family business, so when at the tender age of sixteen years in 1805, by a codicil in his father's will of the time, he is cut out of the will and the family firm, **one wonders what a sixteen-year-old could have done to deserve such treatment.**

In 1805, a William, referred to by the family in wills as "nephew William" and only by outsiders as William Enderby, first appears in the family, according to an anonymous letter in Sam III's granddaughter, Helen Clarke Moffit, nee Gordon's papers.

Mary Enderby still admired Caroline Amelia Elizabeth, Princess of Wales, as in 1808 she had another daughter, which she named Amelia.

Nephew William does not have anything to do with the family firm, his name does not appear on any firm's papers. Had he been the child of Samuel and Mary, he should and would have been on the firm's papers and eventually part owner along with his "brothers" George, Charles and Henry. I can find no clue as to what William Enderby did to earn a living. Census and marriage documents say in reply to occupation that he was a Gentleman, in other words he did not have to work. The 1841 and 1851 censuses of Scotland show a William Enderby with wife, Mary, daughter, Fanny, and sons, William and Charles, and youngest, Elizabeth, living in Inverness with servants. So although no official documentation for William has been found, he is mentioned by outsiders and by the family.

From Ancestry on the net I have extracted the following; - Census *1841 Township of Inverness, Scotland.*

William Enderby	*born about 1806, England.*
Charles Enderby age 4	**born 1837 third born**
Elizabeth Enderby age 2	**born 1839 fourth born**
Fanny Enderby age 9	**born 1832 firstborn**
Mary Enderby age 30	**born 1811 mother**
William Enderby age 35	**born 1805 father**
William Enderby age 6	**born 1835 second born**
Georgina Geham age 15	*live in servants?*
Lillas McLinnen age 20	
Isabel Munro age 30	
Jean Traver age 25	

---

* * *

Beaumont, a Greenwich historian, states that William Enderby and Mary Howls were married in 1830, having eight children. Baptism entry, St. Luke's Church, Charlton, –May 23 1837 Charles, son of William and Mary Enderby. Abode: Eltham. Father's Profession: Gentleman.

Henry Enderby is suspected to have had a dalliance with a Mrs. Eaton, her husband carrying the same name as a founder of the Massachusetts Bay Company. A child resulted named Henry Eaton, who becomes a Silk Merchant, MP and Baron for Chesylmore near Coventry, marries an American, the family of whom is known to the Enderbys and who owned the ship the last Tea Party was held on in Greenwich, Massachusetts, United States; he has a son and names him Henry **Enderby** Eaton. *Henry Enderby is not cut out of the firm or his father's will.*

Mrs. Sam III, Mary Goodwyn, was born in 1767, therefore one year older than her neighbour, **Caroline Amelia** Elizabeth, Princess of Wales. Mary has eight children. Princess Caroline arrives to live in Montagu House, near to Mary's own Loretta House, in 1798, until she leaves in 1814. In those sixteen years, Mary has three daughters and two sons; of the three daughters, two are named **Caroline [b. 1804] and Amelia [b. 1808]**. Neither are family names, Amelia being spelt differently from long time friend Emelia Vansittart at No. 60 Cooms Hill. The third daughter, born in 1802, takes the mother's own name, and a family name for generations: Mary. As time goes on, it is apparent that Amelia is not normal in growth, and remains the height of a twelve year old. Mentally she is as bright as a button, and is the only child of Sam and Mary to see the twentieth century; she is known in the family as Aunt Amy and is the last Enderby to have King Henry VIII's and Catherine of Aragon's bed.

Did **Caroline Amelia**, Princess of Wales, take a special interest in **Amelia** Enderby? The Enderbys are publicity shy; any information has to be dug for—note "We never dine out" in Mary Enderby's letter quoted above. Family letters say how interesting Sunday dinners were, where any Enderby captain in port could attend with a guest.

The Princess of Wales likes children; she is starved of affection, and is bored, with time on her hands. Her neighbour is of her own age with young children and has a brother and sister next door to her with an orphanage, young children galore! What would be more natural for her than to socialise with her neighbours?

In being responsible for the welfare of a number of children, was she copying this childless Enderby couple, whose raising of Anna Maria King before and after her father's death was emulated in William Austin?

Are the children that the Princess of Wales is supposed to have under her care being mixed up by historians and people of the time with the Enderby orphanage? William Austin is a Deptford Dockyard worker's son, and took up residence with the Princess of Wales on 15 November 1802 when a few months old.

The Enderbys cannot be said to be Royalists as their support for the Puritans during the British Civil War testifies. Princess Caroline's non-Royal attitude may have mollified Sam III's opinion of her. Daniel Enderby [1600-1660?] raised Finance

Ordinances in the "Long Parliament" of Oliver Cromwell in 1643 for the army; he may have ended his life on the scaffold for that offence when Charles II was restored to the throne in 1660.

The neckerchief [which can be seen on the net, under Samuel Enderby] is nothing like the other neckerchiefs worn by other sailors illustrated in oil paintings of the Battle of Trafalgar; it is more fitting as a non-ostentatious present from a queen to a youthful lover. In the centre, it is block printed with SE. Looking at the photograph on the net closely, it can be seen that the neckerchief has been neatly repaired; the museum has Samuel IV's darning kit, but it is nice to think the Princess would have been only too pleased to do the mending. Samuel IV's mother, Mary, wife of a ship-owner, would have known not to give a neckerchief like this one to a midshipman, setting him apart from his comrades and making him a target for enemy sharpshooters in the riggings. Nelson is said to have made himself a target by wearing full uniform together with his military decorations and his eye patch; he paid the price.

Lady Ann Hamilton became a friend and a Lady In Waiting to the Princess. Ann should not be confused with Lady Emma Hamilton, mother of Nelson's daughter, Horatia, born in Merton Abbey Gatehouse that was owned by Mrs. James Cook at her death.

Sam IV would appear to be on his own resources. The following I have been able to find from a variety of sources; Samuel IV goes into the Army, as most of his legitimate male descendants have done. According to The Gentleman's Magazine, p. 439, in a list of Defence Force Personnel being retired or placed on half pay:

No. 98—Captain Enderby served with the 22nd Light Dragoons at Belgaum and Sholapore in 1818 and with the 16th Lancers at Bhudapore in 1825-6. In addition to the above, he served three years in the Royal Navy as a Midshipman and was onboard HMS Defence at the battle of Trafalgar.

Samuel was on half pay from 17 February 1832. Half pay for a Captain was 7/6 per day; daily pay for a Captain 14/7.

Verification is stated by the Net to be MONARCH VOIR, whatever that means. Voir is a legal expression for true; Voir: an old French word which signifies the same as the modern word—vrai—true. What does the Monarch portion mean?

Voir Dire, to speak truly, to tell the truth—Anglo-French Noun. The Gentleman's Magazine also says: Enderby, Samuel, York Chasseurs, Ensign 31 Oct. 1811; Lieutenant 16 April 1812; Captain 27 May 1819. The National Archives replied to my query:

> Dear Mr Dawson
> This means [MONARCH VOIR] that he joined his present ship (HMS Defence) which fought at Trafalgar from HMS Monarch where he was a volunteer.
> > Yours sincerely
> > Adrian Ailes
> > Michael McGrady
> > Remote Enquiries Duty Officer

In the York Chasseurs, the rank and file was made up from soldiers that had been in trouble one way or another—officers too? It would not be classed as a desirable regiment, therefore easier to get a commission in, which normally could be purchased for about £3,000. Samuel IV was a first class volunteer aboard HMS Defence at the battle of Trafalgar in June 1805; he has a Phurtpoor [cannot find out what this means] from the 16th Lancers, the Queens Lancers, motto **Death or Glory**. The Lancers followed their nickname and spoke up for the queen, when King George IV heard of this he had them sent to India in June 1822 where they remained for twenty-four years.

Samuel IV married twice; *The first was to Mary Whyte, the daughter of Francis Whyte of Redhills, Ireland, who married Capt. Samuel Enderby, 5th Dragoon Guards, eldest son of Samuel Enderby, Esq. of Blackheath, and has an only daughter Georgian-Mary, Heiress of the estates of the Whytes of Redhill* (from Heraldic illustrations by J. and J.B. Burke). According to the Gentlemen's Magazine of 1847: *A Georgina Mary Enderby, the only daughter of Capt. Enderby, late of the 16th Lancers, was married June 1847 at Bath, Somerset, to the Rev. James Burke Venables, 2nd son of Rev. James Venables of Buckland Newton, Dorset.* The second wife went by the name Emma Jamina, not well thought of by the Enderbys; she wrote to Sir Henry Gordon after Charles Gordon's death (Gordon of Khartoum) asking for money after she had remarried. Samuel IV's Regiments appear to have been: 16th Lancers, 22nd Light Dragoons, York Chasseurs, and 5th Dragoon Guards.

There would be plenty of children running around Crooms Hill. Sam and Mary would have had seven children under the age of sixteen, and the orphanage children, probably under the age of ten. [Many went into the navy, merchant and marine. One orphan was named Potter who returned as a ghost, after falling from the masthead.] Emelia Vansittart had seven older children, then there would be Gov. King's children at various school holiday times and the Goodwyn children across the road.

After the Napoleonic Wars, Samuel Enderby III took his daughter, Elizabeth, and her husband, Captain Gordon, on a Coach holiday to France in 1815. William would be about ten or eleven; his future had to be determined—which school was he to go to [which did he in fact attend]? Why did the daughter and husband go and not his wife? There would be sufficient relations to look after the Enderby children; probably most would be at boarding school. Samuel III's will is not generous towards his wife, for instance he only gives her one year to live in the family house. Caroline, Princess of Wales was on the continent at the same time; 1815 was spent around Lake Como.

Elizabeth and Henry Gordon would appear to be more business confidantes than Sam III's other sons and daughters were; Henry Gordon represents Sam III in Boston, Mass. at the 200th anniversary dinner in 1829 of the Massachusetts Bay Co. landing in America. Sons Charles II, age thirty-one, Henry, age twenty-eight, and George II, age thirty-five, could have gone but did not. An official army tour of Nova Scotia, America and Canada was arranged instead, Captain Gordon having letters of introduction to his Boston hosts who were Otis, thrice mayor of Boston, son of Independence agitator and the son of the Declaration of Independence signer Treat Payne.

When the Prince of Wales met Caroline, he accused her of

being bodily dirty; what he probably meant was that the body odours were not covered up by perfumes and powders as his were. It is ironic that the *only* thing left in England of this Queen of England is her Roman type bath that was in the grounds of Montagu House, Greenwich Park.

The Prince of Wales not knowing of its existence or it would surely have gone the same way as the houses, the bath has recently been renovated and maintained by the people of Greenwich. The bath is not in the grounds of the existing Montagu House, [built in the 1830s] the former grounds being more extensive than now.

From the book "Defence of the Queen," p. 458, "Lord D'Acre arose amidst vehement cries of order and as soon as the peers had taken their seats, he observed, that he had been intrusted with a petition from her majesty praying to be heard by council against the passing of the bill [much cheering] *Lord D'Acre was of the Champion family of Whalers.*"

Caroline arrived for the Coronation in a coach pulled by six beautiful bay horses, elegantly caparisoned , accompanied by Lady Hood and Lady *Ann* Hamilton. Another carriage followed drawn by two horses and containing Lord Hood and Hon. Keppel Craven. *[Lord Hood is Admiral Hood, distant relation to Samuel III's Uncle William Hood, father of English Law.]*

After the queen's return from the continent, she lived in Brandenburgh House, South Audley St., where she died attended by doctors Ainslie, Maton, Warren and Holland; Dr. Lushington is a doctor of law, the queen's legal advisor. After the death of Caroline, the vindictive King George IV demolished this house.

From the 1803 book, "The Beauties of England": *On that part of Blackheath, adjoining to the west side of Greenwich Park, are several villas, one of which, an irregular brick building, whitened over, is now the residence of her Royal Highness, The Princess of Wales. This house had been previously inhabited by the late Duke of Buccleaugh, and before that, by the late Duke of Montagu, from whom, the space included between a double row of trees, and the several mansions on this spot, has obtained the name Montagu Walk. The princess has recently enlarged her little demesne by uniting with it a few acres inclosed from the Park, nearly adjacent is Chesterfield House, purchased in 1753 by Philip, Earl of Chesterfield.* [Stanhope Family]

In 2008, the walk is now known as Chesterfield Walk.

* * *

When Caroline Princess of Wales left Britain in 1814 for the Continent, she was transported to Brunswick in His Majesty's Ship, Jansen, which was stationed in the English Channel to ferry notables in either direction after the fall of Napoleon. The Hon. James King was Captain of the Jansen. He is the Hon. because the Captain was the youngest son of the second Earl of Kingston, of the Irish peerage. Unlike James Cook, he received rapid promotion in the navy; being born in 1784, he joined the navy in 1797, lieutenant in 1804, Commander in 1806, Post Captain in 1809.

The following letter from the Duke of Clarence was received by Captain Hon. James King, Commanding Officer of HMS Jason on about 5 August 1814. It is reported that he read it at breakfast in the presence of his surgeon, James Hall. The use of capital letters is believed to be the same as in the original.

Dear King,

You are going to be ordered to take the Princess of Wales to the Continent. If you DON'T COMMIT ADULTERY WITH HER, YOU ARE A DAMNED FOOL! You have my consent for it and I can assure you that you have that of MY BROTHER THE REGENT.

> Yours
> (Duke of Clarence)

A largely unknown letter. The morals of this Royal Family left a lot to be desired. *Captain and Doctor retired to the same locality in Kent.*

Possibly the least biased description of Caroline is by the above mentioned surgeon James Hall;-*The Royal Standard was lowered, and we now only await a fair wind. Her Royal Highness is about five feet 3 inches in height, her features masculine – her eyes small, her countenance is cheerful – she has small feet, but her legs and body are of great size – Her accent is bad, inclining to the German. Her temper appears to be cheerful. She has declared to her friends that she had received so much pleasure from this voyage and has been so very happy in this ship, that she regrets leaving us. She has requested Captain K. will accept a piece of plate; to the crew she has left one hundred pounds, and to the band she has given thirty – On the whole this voyage has been very agreeable to all parties.*

In many ways Caroline was like her half niece(?) Queen Victoria.

* * *

The Prince of Wales [George IV] was shot at with a rifle, after the opening of Parliament in 1817. Carriage windows were broken—not to be wondered at, in view of the above letter.

* * *

Samuel Enderby's House, 68 Crooms Hill, Blackheath, is now the Presbytery for the Catholic Church next door, which was built in the garden of Sam's House. Charles and Elizabeth Enderby's orphanage next door has gone in the passage of time. Sam's house was partly constructed from materials salvaged from the demolition of Wricklemarsh Manor on Blackheath; they would seem keen on demolition in that era.

When Sandwich's House(s) were demolished in 1815, after Caroline's 1814 departure for the Continent, "the Old Mill" was demolished also. Both these buildings are shown in an incorrect relationship in a painting owned by the city of London, when compared with the 1794 plan of Blackheath Hundred.

The existing Montagu House, next door to the Presbytery, is of 1830s vintage, lovingly repaired after V1 and V2 damage during World War II. This house is often represented as the original Montagu House, in spite of the fact of demolition, it being more presentable than the Earls one or two houses at the southwest corner of Greenwich Park. The owner/designer of the existing Montagu House at 70 Crooms Hill must have been interested in history, first to name it Montagu and secondly, to design/build the house reminiscent of those that were demolished; the "circular room" continues. It is notable that neither the Earl's house site nor the Old Mill site is built on today, the later being a desirable site. There is a Montague House not far away, once an orphanage, which should not be mistaken for the Earl of Sandwich's House(s) which were demolished.

Could William Enderby have pushed his claim to the British Throne when William IV succeeded to the throne in 1830 or when his *niece* Victoria did in 1837?

William was a brother of George IV with no legitimate children, ten little bastards running around, and two daughters with his wife, Queen Adelaide of Saxe Coburg, who died in infancy.

Why did William Enderby go to Inverness to live? Just about as far from London as possible to go and still be in society. Dundee was the whaling port.

Peculiar how history repeats itself.

GRAVE STONE OF SAMUEL ENDERBY IV

Photo by Tony Coombe
St. Teilo's Church Graveyard, Llandeilo, Carmarthenshire, Wales.

Samuel Enderby IV according to the Goodwyn Genealogy in America, had 4 wives, the first was Mary Maxwell who died at Greenwich 31st March 1815. The second was Rebeca Davis born 22 Oct. 1789 who died at Madras, leaving issue[?]. The third wife was Mary Whyte heiress to Redhill estates in Ireland.

The fourth wife is Emma Jamima Carver of Llandeilo, Wales. They were married in St. Stephens Church Paddington, London, on 17th October 1868. Samuel would be 79 having been born in 1789 and Emma was 26 years old. Emma remarried the same year of Samuel IV's death.

THE WHEATLEY'S AT THE
BOSTON TEA PARTY

In the middle of the eighteenth century, two baby girls were born in vastly different circumstances. Their paths were destined to cross and join for a time; their union would be at a pleasant time for both, during which, they would be witness to events having world significance and effect.

The eldest of the two was born around 1753 in a country with no known borders, no known name, but approximates to today's Senegal, Africa. The newborn babe was given no known name, and her parents are unknown. It can only be assumed that they loved and provided for her to the extent that she was a worthy prize for slave traders, who captured her at the age of about seven and transported her to the market at Boston, Massachusetts, United States.

In Boston, an area of North America that was colonised in the early 1600s by Europeans of dissenting religions, mainly of Evangelical Protestant persuasions, there lived John Wheatley, a *master tailor*, "a good man" (as the saying goes) meaning one who did not cheat, maltreat his fellow man, treated the opposite sex with respect and acknowledged that they had a mind and brain. The Wheatley family consisted of parents, mother Susanna, twin son and daughter, Nathaniel and Mary;

Mrs. Wheatley was not in good health so the family agree to engage a maidservant to her. The Wheatleys were beginning not to agree with slavery; there had been a lot of discussion of how to go about getting a maidservant—should they employ a local girl or purchase a slave? A purchase would mean at least one saved from the deprivations that many slaves underwent, but the purchase would encourage the ill-gotten trade. What exactly decided the Wheatleys to purchase a slave, and why did they go to the market the day that this young female was for sale or why they purchased her, a purchase that was not to be regretted by anyone, we do not know.

Upon arriving home, the first thing that was done was to give her a wash down in the scullery before she entered the house. Whether she had ever had a wash before is not known, but a slave trading ship did not have water to spare for ablutions, maybe the time to throw a bucket of sea water over them; accommodation was crowded so insects and disease were easily transmitted from one person to another. Possibly they had been better fed for a few days before reaching port; also an attempt to smarten them up prior to sale may have been done.

The second and third things were to give her some clothes and to reassure her that she was not going to be ill-treated. How you did this to a seven-year-old girl who had just been through the ordeal of a two-month sea voyage in the conditions prevailing, I do not know. The clothing would be necessary because Boston, Mass., would never be as warm as Senegal; it could possibly be the first time she had had any form of clothing on. The sight of the two Wheatley ladies wearing similar clothes and the warmth from the clothes may have been the only comforting things to her, not having vocal understanding between them. Fourthly, would be to give her food and drink, during the consuming of which, a name for her could have been discussed; Phillis was chosen, possibly the name of the ship she came to Boston on.

The Wheatleys treated Phillis as a daughter and sister. This treatment of a young Negress probably raised a few eyebrows amongst the general population; abolition of slavery was still years ahead. Phillis's demeanour and ability may well have hurried things on. Mrs. Wheatley, helped by her daughter, Mary, taught Phillis reading, writing and speaking English before she was ten years old. The ability to read and write by the age of ten was not accomplished by many Boston born children; many adults never did.

During the first years, it must have been noticed by the Wheatley family that Phillis had ability, a gift for learning, which was encouraged so that in the next two years, she could read and write in Latin as well as English. Latin may have been taught by Nathaniel as he is the only one who went to a school where it is known to have been taught. A gift Phillis had, but she must have had good teachers as well, who must have been able to do what they taught.

By 1766, the best estimates that could be made put Phillis at thirteen years of age; she was a local celebrity and beginning to attract attention from England and what is known as the Benelux countries, the main trading partners with the port of Boston. Her ability to translate and articulate a story from Ovid astonished local scholars; her voice was strong, clear and pleasant, and led to her singing and giving recitals of poetry. By the age of fourteen, she had composed mature conventional poetry about morality and piety. All of this gives a picture of what the whole Wheatley family *way of living* was like, many years ahead of their time, in respect to the treatment of their fellow man.

Across the Atlantic Ocean on the eighth of November 1757, in London Town, within the hearing of the bells of St. Paul's Cathedral, rebuilt by Wren, paid for by a tax on coal, after the disastrous Great Fire of London in 1666, Mary Enderby was born at Paul's Wharf, which is now Paul's Walk, the northern end of the Millennium Pedestrian Bridge over the River Thames. She was the third child to Samuel Enderby II and his wife Mary Buxton, a sister for Charles I and Samuel III.

Samuel II was described by the London *Times* newspaper upon his death in 1797 as a *"oil and St. Petersburg merchant"*; the oil was from whales, the St. Petersburg merchant description would be because the family business owned shipping and traded with St. Petersburg, on the Russian Baltic coast, being members of the *Muscovy Company*. Samuel II was the spokesperson to the British government on matters concerning the whaling industry and shipping across the Atlantic to the colonies of New England. The family was religious and pious just like the Wheatleys; they would know of each other through their business and religious interests.

Samuel leaving £90,000 in his 1797 will shows the Enderbys did not lack for money; the family had been successful in the leather business for years, assisting the successful Oliver Cromwell in the British Civil War of 1640-1660, receiving Irish lands in exchange. It is unlikely that Mary wanted for anything in her life and would have had the education applicable to someone of her social standing.

Phillis Wheatley was having local success and renown, her first poem, *"An Elegiac Poem, on the death of the Celebrated Divine George Whitfield" was* published in 1770. Knowledge of her and her ability had reached London, an invitation from nobility and academia, prominent among which were the Earl of Dartmouth and the Countess of Huntingdon, for Phillis to visit the city, to sing and give recitals in London in 1772 was received. At that time, a woman could not travel alone on land, never mind the closed confines of a ship, particularly a Negro woman; she had to have a male escort. Phillis continued writing poetry, most with a religious connection, so that by 1773, she had sufficient to compile a book of her poems.

Arrangements were made for her to travel to London in June 1773, accompanied by the son of the family, Nathaniel Wheatley. This they did; the whole expedition being an outstanding success for both of them. Phillis was probably the first academically educated Negro person that London society had been introduced to; it would be hard to find a better example. The idea for the abolition of slavery was getting underway: Phyllis's reception by the London society of the day and the publishing of her well received book, *"Poems on Various Subjects: Religious and Moral,"* in London, by a Mr. Thornton, a bookseller and relation to the Wilberforce anti-slavery family; [*twenty years later he would also be a subscriber to Capt. Phillips Book, about his early years as Governor of Australia*], did no harm to the movement.

The full length portrait of Phillip, the Founding Governor of Australia that most people will remember, was painted in 1786 by Francis Wheately, *son of a London master tailor.* Did Francis Wheatley paint Phillis's portrait in a white gown [bridesmaid's dress?] that surfaced in Paris in the 1830s? Phillis was a slave of John Wheatley who is often described as a *Boston master tailor.*

Nathaniel Wheatley was also enjoying himself as he had met the love of his life in Mary Enderby. Given the similarities that there were in the lifestyles of both families, it is not surprising that Nathaniel should meet fifteen-year-old Mary, who, judging by her subsequent actions, was a mature young woman. Nathaniel and Mary fell in love; he proposed and was accepted by Mary and her parents, three brothers and two sisters. However there was a legal impediment to their marriage: the minimum age for marriage was sixteen years.

Correspondence from Boston, Mass., suggested the failing health of the Wheatley parents, Mrs. Wheatley in particular. This was not good news for either of the two young Wheatleys who naturally wished to be with them. Information from America was five to six weeks old when received, to return to America would take a similar time. It is possible that Phillis travelled back to America by herself, in Enderby ship *Beaver*, under the protection of Captain Coffin, an American of New England from the Coffyn family of Somerset County in Old England, a family who supplied several Enderby captains. In all probability, she would wish to attend her "brother's" wedding, the romance of which she would have seen from the beginning; It is not every day that any young woman, let alone a Negress (in 1773), would be given the chance to see a London society wedding, to say nothing of being the guest of honour as the groom's "sister." However Phillis decided that duty called and so went back to America before the wedding took place. Nathaniel Wheatley, twenty-seven years of age, married sixteen-year-old Mary Enderby in the family Parish Church, of St. Bennet's, Paul's Wharf, on 10 November, 1773.

The autumn of 1773 had been an important time for the bride's father and politically for Great Britain; how important, all were about to find out. For no apparent good reason, it had been decided by the political powers that were, to tax Indian tea sold by the Honourable English East India Company when sold in America, but not on tea sold in Britain. The American Colonies had demonstrated their unwillingness to pay such taxes in the past, so this act can be said to be direct provocation. The colonialists were prepared politically for such an eventuality; people belonging to various religious sects, on both sides of the Atlantic had primed the situation. Benjamin Franklin would have enjoyed the experience, particularly when he was playing chess with the widow of the fourth Lord Howe.

The first such tea was to be transported by four ships:

"The Dartmouth" captained by Hall, owned by American Francis Rotch (1750-1822?), the 1773 Enderby agent in Boston, Mass.

"Eleanor," captained by Bruce, owned by Samuel Enderby and Sons.

"Beaver" captained by Coffin, owned by Samuel Enderby and Sons. Captain Part Owner? The fourth ship, "William," captained by Loring, was lost on Cape Cod; but not its 50 chests of tea, which were the only ones deposited in Boston Castle.

Photo by A.A. Dawson
St. Bennets

Newspapers, Massachusetts Gazette and Boston Weekly Newsletter, confirm ships Captains were Hall, Bruce and Coffin as does a Boston Tea Party handbill of 2 Dec. 1773. The tea is reputed to have been owned by Davison and Newman. The Tea Party ships sailed down the Thames River on 10 November 1773, with the two Wheatleys catching the *Beaver* at Deal in the county of Kent. Ships travelled slowly down the Thames; wind and tide flow could be against the ship.

The loss of one ship indicates the Atlantic crossing was no picnic. *The Dartmouth* made good time; the first to enter port on Sunday 28 November 1773 and tied up to *Griffins Wharf*— not the usual wharf for ships from London. Is this evidence of collusion? The regulations gave a ship's captain/agent twenty days after entering port or upon unloading the tea, to pay the taxes owing: *Dartmouth* to pay up by 17 December.

Eleanor was at *Griffins Wharf* on 2 December. Duties payable by 22 December. Rotch, Enderby Agent, is therefore the spokesperson for all three ships. This was convenient to say the least. Americans do not appear to question why just Francis Rotch is questioned about all three ships. *Beaver* does not tie up to the wharf until after the tea party; she has been tied up to the Quarantine station since 7 December because of a non-existent smallpox case, a ruse to keep Mary Wheatley out of the expected trouble over refusal to pay the tea tax? The fact that initially there were only two ships at Griffins Wharfe is borne out by the statement of Tea Party participant Ebenezer Stevens who said, "I commanded with a party on board the vessel of which Alexander Hodgdon was mate, and as he knew me, I left that vessel with some of my comrades, and went on board the other vessel which lay at the opposite side of the wharf." So there were only two vessels at Griffins Wharf, which appears to have been a finger wharf. Alexander Hodgdon was mate aboard *Dartmouth*. Ebenezer married Rebecca Hodgdon 11 November 1774.

The Tea Party took place in the evening of 16 December 1773, just before *Dartmouth* was to pay the tax. More than one American account of the Party mentions that one ship was unusually well loaded with goods. Could these have been Nathaniel's and Samuel III's goods paid for by Samuel Enderby II as stated in his Will?

The wait at the quarantine station would have been frustrating for Nathaniel, anxious to see his mother. Messages passed to the quarantine station did not alleviate their anxiety. Nathaniel was in the know but that knowledge did not assist him; he had an unknown bride to introduce to the family and friends, and to set himself up as the agent for the Enderby's, also a large quantity of goods to set himself up in business with his new brother in law, Samuel Enderby III, being the partner in Europe procuring goods for sale in "*America and the South.*"

Mrs. Wheatley Sr. died early in 1774 knowing that Phillis had had a success and that a grandchild was on the way. Mr. Wheatley Sr. died in 1778 when gunfire was being heard; Nathaniel's twin sister, Mary, dyed shortly after, having married the Rev. Lathrop in 1771. That left the three Wheatleys, Nathaniel, his wife Mary, and Phillis, on their own to face the oncoming troubles of a civil war that was to last eight long years before a Peace Treaty would be signed. Is it possible for twins to have a medical condition from which both die at a certain age?

Apart from a Samuel Enderby letter that was intercepted by the British authorities and is now in the National Archives, London, dated December 1775, to Nathaniel at Providence, Rhode Island, a copy of the letter being in the Congress Library, very little is known of him.

Nathaniel had moved from Boston to Providence, because of the British naval blockade of Boston. Nathaniel, Mary with one child, and Phillis, first went to Nantucket in May 1775. This was found by Elizabeth Oldham of Nantucket Historical Society when investigating my request for information on Nathaniel and ship *Hero*.

Nathaniel and Mary had two daughters, Mary and Elizabeth; all three ladies landed in England in 1781, two years before the signing of a peace treaty. The Enderby family leased a house, 14 The Grove, from the Morden College, at Blackheath, Greenwich, London, [*4 the Grove known as the Chocolate House for the owners sold the new confectionary there, often patronized by King George III*] where the rest of the family now lived; this lease was renewed in 1801. It is quite likely that Mary was widowed in the War of Independence. Nathaniel is said to be deceased in the 1796 Will of Samuel Enderby II, but not how or why. Nathaniel is not mentioned again in Enderby family papers. Did the capture of Sam II's December 1775 letter cause Nathaniel's death/disappearance? The last we know of Nathaniel is that his ship, *Hero*, was captured by the British in July 1777, in ballast from Nantucket to France, and sent to Newport, RI.

Naval Documents of the American revolution, Vol.9

Name of	**Hero**
Master of Vessel:	Alexander Coffin
Rig of Vessel	Ship
Date of Capture	31 July 1777
Place of Capture	Off Cape Sable
Captor:	**HM Frigate Flora**
Home Port	
From Where	Nantucket, Massachusetts
To What Place	France
Cargo:	Ballast
Tonnage:	
Battery:	
Crew:	
Owners:	Nathaniel Wheatley
Prize mas	
Prize cr	
Ordered I	
Into Whatport	Newport, Rhode Island
Date Arrival	Newport, Rhode Island
Date Trial	
Date Sold:	
Action:	
No	
Reca	
No	

Comments: Ship *Hero* (Alexander Coffin; owned by Nathaniel Wheatley) was bound from Nantucket, Massachusetts to France in ballast. She was captured on 31 July 1777 by HM Frigate *Flora* and sent in to Newport, Rhode Island.

From *The journal of H.M.S. Flora, Captain John Brisbane.*

July 1777, Connonicut Light House No 70.25 Wt Distance 100 Leagues

Thursday 31 AM at 5 saw a Sail in the SW Standing to the So wd, Out Reefs sett Studing sails and gave Chace, at 10 Fired 2 Six Pounders at the Chace and brother too. Shortene'd Sail, Hoisted out the Cutter and sent an Officer onboard—

First part Modt and fair, Middle fresh winds and hazy Wt, latter fair—PM1/2 past Noon the Cutter retd. The Chace proved the Hero from Nantuckett bound to Old France, got the Prisoners onbd. And sent 2 Petty Officers and 10 Men to take Charge of her, at 4 in Boat and made Sail—Master was Alexander Coffin ship in ballast.

This Alexander Coffin is the senior, about whom little is known; it is his son, Alexander Coffin Jr., who wrote about the prison hulks of New York. Alexander Coffin Sr. is mentioned in Samuel Enderby's intercepted letter of December 1775 as being in London undecided what to do. A hint to Nathaniel?

Samuel Enderby II's 1796 will says that Nathaniel and Samuel III had gone into partnership with Sam II financing the project which made a loss due to the War and Nathaniel's death. The project was for *"Nathaniel to sell goods to America and South"* with Samuel III purchasing and shipping the goods from Britain. In the various accounts of the Boston Tea Party, there are references to a lot of goods aboard one ship.

The Enderbys had a whaler in 1786 that was larger than

usual, named *Hero*—was this Nathaniel's Ship? In New-buryport, Essex County, Massachusetts, Old Hill cemetery near today's Bartlett Mall, is the grave of Ebenezer and John Bradbury. Upon the grave stone is: "Died 1777 lost at sea in the ship *Hero*." Both were young men under twenty. Did the firing of the 2 six pounders cause loss of life aboard *Hero* that was not reported?

During the War of Revolution, the British hired Hessian troops from Germany. Lt. Von Lindau aboard ship *Hero* wrote to his commanding officer, addressing him as His Highness, on 1 August 1783 stating "that we are supposedly to set sail tomorrow"; by the 16th September *Hero* was at "The Downs" which is the narrow part of The English Channel. Is this when the Enderbys laid claim to the ship on behalf of Mary Wheatley nee Enderby who was now living in London, therefore the ship was not a prize of War but a British owned ship? Legalities plus repairs could easily have taken up to 1787 to turn the ship into a whaler for The Southern Whaling Co., after being in the Northern Whaling fleet previously.

In Sam II's will it would appear that Mary Wheatley had money invested in the family firm. She appears to receive more than anyone else and there is a mention of a 1786 £10,000 bond in Mary's favour. Can anyone help with the mystery of Nathaniel's disappearance? Investigations continue, having started in 1989.

After *The Tea Party*, all things went downhill for Phillis; first her mistress died, followed by her master, who fortunately freed her from slavery first, although there is no written proof of this. Then her "sister" Mary Lathrop died, quickly followed by Nathaniel. Phillis married a free Negro, called John Peters in 1778, who turned out to be a good-for-nothing. Phillis had children, but increasing poverty and ill-treatment caused the family to die an obscure death, shortly after the Peace Treaty was signed in 1783. Having no recording equipment in that day, we do not know what her singing was like but the poetry of the first educated Negro slave remains.

Mary and Phillis were witnesses to the very beginning of Samuel Enderby II's *"grand scheme"* [on behalf of the oil industry and financiers] to get British whalers into the Indian and Pacific Oceans, as mentioned in his 1775 intercepted letter to Nathaniel Wheatley, oceans forbidden by the Queen Elizabeth I charter to the Honourable English East India Company, signed on the last day of December in 1600. Samuel's letter to his Agent/Son-in-Law, of December 1775, was intercepted by the British Authorities not American as most historians state. The Library of Congress only has a copy; the original is in the British National Archives, who ran up against the Freedom of Information Act, when, on my behalf, they were trying to ascertain where the letter had been intercepted.

This Freedom of Information refusal after 240 years makes me think I am on the right line of investigation. The Tea party was engineered by parties on both sides of the Atlantic, as was thought at the time by many people.

THE AMERICAN REVOLUTION
by EDWARD COUNTRYMAN

"To the Americans, the notion of conspiracy offered a way to make sense of their troubles; who the conspirators were, remained something of an open question."

The following shows the feeling was on both sides of the Atlantic.

On 10April 1775, The Lord Mayor, Aldermen, and livery of London, in regalia of office and accompanied by the sheriffs, carried an Address, Remonstrance and Petition to St. James Palace. The Petition alleged *"that the Ministry measures originate in the secret advice of men who are enemies equal to your Majesties Title and the Liberties of the people."*

Helen Clarke Moffit, granddaughter of Samuel Enderby III, and sister to the British hero General Gordon of Khartoum, kept the family papers and the model ship; all her papers, Gordon and Enderby, were saved in the British Library upon her death and that of her sister Mary, Mrs. Blunt. *"Military and Naval men, great Lawyers and Statesmen, Lord Mayors of the City of London and over rich Bankers obtain high rank and renown, but I do not think leaving out the connection of the Enderby's with America, that any have more right to be proud of the part they have played in the world than have the Enderby's"* is an excerpt from the anonymous 1875 letter, found in Mrs. Moffit's papers, a copy of which is in the Mitchell Library Sydney. Helen, Mrs. Moffit, married Dr. Moffit, Gordon's medical colleague in the Chinese Opium Wars.

Very little happens in history that is unconnected with something else. Coincidently(?) Rhode Island is where the renamed *Endeavour* ended up during the War of Revolution. *Endeavour* being the ship of Capt. James Cook when he discovered the east coast of Australia, believed to have been renamed *Sandwich*. The Earl of Sandwich, a First Lord of the Admiralty [boss of the British Royal Navy] being a neighbour of Samuel Enderby III, who had a few ships named for his neighbour. Sam's whalers also named the Namibian port of Sandwich in Africa after the Earl.

The Royal Navy did not have a Fleet of ships in a time of peace and was therefore short of money and employment when the *Endeavour* was originally purchased, altered twice, victualed and readied for a three year voyage in record time, which is not done without money being available and plenty of it. The speed with which it was done in the Naval Dockyard at Deptford near Greenwich shows that the dockyard was not busy. Who better than the head of the whaling industry and financial backers of the oil industry of the day, to put up the money for a ship going where the British whalers were forbidden to go, so that the talk by East Indiamen crews of whales galore could be verified? It is significant that whales are hardly mentioned by Cook, the only commercial object in the two oceans, which were abundant. At the time of *Endeavour* sailing, British included any American whalers that were not owned by English concerns. The intercepted letter shows that ships thought to be American owned were not and that Sam Enderby could and did give orders for ships not belonging to him.

There is no record of King George III ever having paid his promised £4,000 towards *Endeavour's* cost but someone [George III or Government department?] placed *American* "Matra"—"Magra" or McGrath aboard the *Endeavour* as a James Bond kind of spy. The British Government have records for this gentleman in both names, Matra and Magra. He became the British Consul in Tunis.

Massachusetts Governor Hutchinson, in his 1828 book on the History of the Massachusetts Bay Company, [*200th anniversary of landing in America; at the commemorative dinner at Nahant, on Wednesday August 12, 1829, Samuel Enderby III was represented and was a toast*] says the following of an unidentified ship that comes into port after *Dartmouth*, (only Enderby ships), "*Another vessel had also arrived from London, with 28 chests of tea on account of the merchants. The owners of the vessel were friends to liberty, and caused her to be carried to the same wharf where the other tea ships had lain; and, the first night after her arrival, the tea was taken out by people disguised, and thrown into the sea; and the vessel hauled the next day to the wharf where vessels from London usually unlade, to take out the rest of her lading.*"

Hutchinson, by using the word *other*, which means more than one, also the plural for ship, must have been referring to *Beaver*. This statement of Hutchinson agrees with that of Ebenezer Stevens, which is a rare occurrence with American descriptions of the Tea Party.

What Mary saw was the beginning of a Protestant European colony in Australia repeating the American experience of Massachusetts Bay Co. To facilitate the replenishing of whalers on a three-year voyage to seas—shown by the whaling industry financed *Endeavour* voyage—that were teaming with whales to the extent that when Thomas Melvill, in Enderby ship *Britannia*, caught and extracted oil from the first Australian whale, to provide Australia's first export, he could write to his employers: "*We sailed through different shoals of them from 12 o'clock in the day till sunset, all around the horizon, as far as I could see from the mast head."* **Yet Cook sailed the east coast of Australia during months that are now whale watching months and never recorded seeing a whale along the coast.**

The *Brittania* letter was three years after the Enderby ship *Emelia* [on maiden voyage and named after Emelia Vansittart] had become the first **known** whaler or British commercial ship rounding Cape Horn into the Pacific, in the Australian First Fleet year of **1788**, (also the route of Cook's *Endeavour,* and *Drakes Golden Hind*) filled her holds with Spermaceti oil and got back to London claiming the British Government prize of £800 for so doing. The Captain Jas Shields, and Archelus Hammond, harpoonist, were Americans from Nantucket. This is five years after the signing of the Peace Treaty of 1783. I suspect that these Americans worked on British whalers *after* the war because of the decimation of the American whaling fleet, to earn money to start again. The rapid growth of the American fleet of whalers was such that financial assistance had to have been obtained from somewhere.

The same Thomas Melvill was Captain of the Enderby ship *Friendship,* which was the second legal British whaler around Cape Horn in 1789 to claim the prize of £700. This Thomas Melvill is not the grandfather of Herman Melville the author; he is a Londoner who captained Enderby ships before settling in Cape Town.

British whalers claimed that the Elizabethan charter did not say anything about going west of Cape Horn, [bottom of South America] only forbidding going east of Cape of Good Hope [Cape Town]. The first Elizabethans did not realise that both led to the same place, even though Francis Drake, the first Captain to circumnavigate the world, had done exploring in the *unknown* [to the British] Pacific via Cape Horn 200 years before Cook ventured into a known, [comparative to Drake] Pacific.

Hermann Melville in his book *Moby Dick* could say: *"The ship was named after the late Samuel Enderby, Merchant of London, the original of the famous whaling house of Enderby and Sons, a house which in my poor whaleman's opinion, comes not far behind the united Royal houses of Tudors and Bourbons, in point of real historical interest."*

A model of the ship, *Samuel Enderby*, made by the shipbuilder's son, seen by the author when a little boy visiting his Enderby grandparents at Boston, Lincolnshire, England, caused the author to do this research. The model of the ship *Samuel Enderby* is now in the Maritime Museum, Greenwich, England, just down Crooms [Cooms] Hill from where Samuel Enderby III lived.

Herman Melville in his 1851 book, *Moby Dick*, has this to say about Australia: *"That great America on the other side of the sphere, Australia, was given to the enlightened world by the whaleman. After its first blunder –born discovery by a Dutchman; all other ships long shunned those shores as pestiferously barbarous; but the whale ship touched there. The whale ship is the true mother of that now mighty colony. Moreover, in the infancy of the first Australian settlement, the emigrants were several times saved from starvation by the benevolent 'biscuit' of the whale ship luckily dropping an anchor in their waters."*

The ship *Samuel Enderby* and the Enderbys constitute chapters 100 and 101 of *Moby Dick*, which is the most that I have found in writing about the Enderbys. Note: Benjamin Franklin is in London as agent for Massachusetts when Phillis Wheatley, a Negro slave, and her "brother" Nathaniel Wheatley, both from Boston, Massachusetts, are there in 1773, Phillis to give singing and recital concerts at the request of the Earl of Dartmouth and the Countess of Huntingdon, both having financial interests in New England. Benjamin Franklin's mother was a Folger of Nantucket; W. Folger was captain of Enderby whaler *Experiment* in 1777 and 1778, after the start of the War of Independence and of ship *Hero* after the War of Revolution. The Wheatleys, Enderbys and Franklyn must have known each other and had dealings with each other, yet there is no known correspondence between them.

Benjamin Franklin's favourite coffee house is said to have been in "St. Paul's Churchyard;" this is generally thought of as being the area in front of St. Paul's Cathedral. This is possibly incorrect; the churchyard being the area of land the St. Peters Church occupied when it was burnt down in the fire of London in 1666. This churchyard is within metres of Samuel II's abode and place of work at St. Paul's Wharf, Lower Thames Street. I have found the following: "**St Peter, Paul's Wharf,** *Upper Thames Street.* First mentioned in 1170 as St. Peter the Little. Stow described it as '*a small parish church . . . no monuments do remain.*' A churchyard had been added in 1430, the gift of one **Robert Frankelyn**. In 1625 and 1655 the church was repaired. *Church burnt down in 1666, "The Great Fire of London"* Lambeth Palace Library, London, H.Q. of the Church of England, assure me that (a marriage allegation, dated 30 October, 1773) for the marriage licence of Nathaniel Wheatley and Mary Enderby, for their wedding which took place 11days later. This document confirms that Nathaniel Wheatley was a bachelor of the parish of Greenwich, and that Mary Enderby was a minor of the parish of St Peter, Paul's Wharfe, London. It also states, however, that the couple were free to marry in either of the parish churches aforesaid.

The e-mail goes on to say that the parish register of St. Paul's Wharfe is held at the Guildhall Library, while those of Greenwich are held at the London Metropolitan Archives. The 1841 census shows Wheatleys, coachbuilders, residing in Greenwich.

From The Gentleman's Magazine for November 1773
See the wedding on the 13th lucky for some!

Stewart Gillies, reference Team Manager at the British Library, Newspapers, says that the General Evening Post, 11 November 1773, states: *"Married yesterday, at St. Bennet's Paul's Wharf, Mr. Nathaniel Wheatley, of Boston, New England, to Miss Enderby, of Thames St"* Gillies points out that it was not the custom to give a wedding a write up, stating the guests attending, which is a pity as a list would have been informative. Newspapers etc. at that time were not printed for females to read, hence the name "Gentleman's Magazine."

After the church of St. Peters, Paul's Wharfe, was burnt down, the church authorities used the area for retail. Freemasons, rejuvenated in 1717, met in four London pubs, *The Goose and Gridiron* in St Paul's churchyard was one.

Captain Gordon represented his father-in-law, Samuel Enderby III, at the 200th anniversary dinner of the first landing of the Massachusetts Bay Company in America, Samuel being a toast at the dinner in a hotel in Nahant near Boston, on Wednesday 12 August 1829, a date that fits the criteria for meetings laid down in the Massachusetts Bay Act. His hosts and guides were H.G. Otis, Mayor of Boston, and Treat Payne, son of a signer of the Declaration of Independence. Otis would be starting the first of three terms as Mayor of Boston. *[Otis Elevators are made by the same family.]* No Samuel Enderby is known to have visited America, so why would these two prominent Americans host his son-in-law who was on an official(!) Army Tour of New England and Canada and therefore should be in army uniform. Thankfully, he left a daily report of his tour.

I was pleased to be able to tell Glasgow University the significance of a book they have in their library. Charles Enderby

I and Samuel Enderby III gave to their sister, Mary, on her wedding day a leather bound book of Dr. Arne's Musical Manuscripts, amongst which is his music for *Rule Brittania*; also in the book is the manuscript for a song called *Young Phillis One Morning* (that spelling of Phyllis is not usual in Britain). The music and song is probably the work of Michael Arne, the doctor's son, although Glasgow University attributes it to a Mr. Worgan or Boyce. Mr. Worgan was the father of Surgeon Worgan of the First Fleet to Australia, who took a piano with him leaving it to Mrs. MacArthur. Dr. Arne taught Charles Burney, musical historian, father of author and diarist Fanny Burney and James Burney who sailed with Cook, also the daughter Sussana, who married Molesworth Phillips, who was an avenger for and a witness to Capt. Cook's killing. Reverend Dr. Charles Burney Jr. had a school in Greenwich; he is also remembered in George Enderby's Will. Glasgow University said they have not got the personnel to transcribe the words and music, which is a pity.

A Phillis Wheatley poem dedicated to the Countess of Huntingdon is signed BOSTON JUNE 12- 1773, indicating the Wheatley's did not leave Boston until *after* that date. Preface to Phillis's book has an oval, side view of Phillis, surrounded by the wording:

Negro Servant of John Wheatley,
Printed for A. Bell bookseller, Aldgate.
Sold by Messrs. COX and BERRY, King St. Boston MD
   CC LXXIII.
Published according to Act of Parliament Sept. 1st 1773 by
   Arch. Bell, Bookseller No.8 near The Saracens Head.

Still—in Boston 12 June, book published 1 September, 5 week voyage across Atlantic—they did not let grass grow under their feet. Phillis's poem: "Farewell to America and Mrs. SW" dated Boston May 7 1773 seems to be saying farewell *from* a ship to Mrs. SW and America.

St. Bennets (or Benet depending what era) other claims to fame are that Shakespeare lived close by and probably attended services there. It is now the Welsh church for London. For centuries it has been the church for the College of Heraldry. Wren designed it; it is unusual in that it is constructed from red and blue bricks with white quoin and window stone. The interior is almost square.

Large industries plot and scheme, yesterday and today.

Paul's Wharf is now Paul's Walk, on the Northern bank of the River Thames, below the Millennium Pedestrian Suspension Bridge. Can be seen on Google Earth.

I found on the net facsimiles of Phillis's letters dated 18 and 30 October 1773, apparently from Boston to people in America, indicating she returned to America before Nathaniel and Mary were married. The Massachusetts History Society website published Phillis's correspondence dated Boston, October 1773.

If they left Boston on the Wheatley's *London* in June, it would have only just returned to Boston when Phillis received in the city of London the command to return, at about the end of August, having landed in London mid-July. To write a letter in Boston on 18 October, Phillis would have had to leave London before September, or she would have attended the publishing of her book, which she did not.

	Ship London	
BOSTON	5 week voyage	LONDON
Left mid June		arrived end of July
Arrived end of August		arrived end of September
Assuming straight turnaround, no delays.		

I think Mrs Sussanah Wheatley may have been a selfish woman, if she did request her to return. For nearly two years, the Wheatleys had been talking about Phillis going to London. What she had done for Phillis does not suggest a selfish person. If help was required by the senior Wheatleys, could not temporary assistance have been found? What did they do for the ten weeks plus for Phillis to get to Boston? Phillis would not have reached London when the request to return was sent. Mrs. Wheatley would know that Phillis could not arrive in America before, at least, ten weeks after posting the letter.

There is *no proof* of emancipation of Phillis by John Wheatley, just a mention of it in a letter by Phillis to a friend. In the same letter, she mentions that Mr. Hall will be in Boston on 28 October when Capt. Hall, of Rotch's ship Dartmouth, did not get in until 28 November. If the Halls are the same, it would indicate a postponed sailing in London.

There is on the net information about Nathaniel getting married for which they cannot have any proof. The facts are as set out above. The mystery as to what happened to Nathaniel is deepened by Phillis's correspondence, which states: *whilst she is in Providence R.I.* [living with Nathaniel and Mary

Wheatley? Boston History Society thinking that Mary Wheatley is Nathaniel's sister who should have been known as Mary Lathrop, not knowing that it is his wife] *she writes a covering note to George Washington at Cambridge on 25 (26?) October 1775, which reaches Washington in Mid December 1775 and is published in the Virginia Gazette on March 20 1776, Washington refers to Phillis's poem in correspondence to his Adjutant Joseph Reed on 10 February 1776.* Washington's letter dated 28 February 1776 invites Phillis to his HQ in Cambridge, which she does a few days before the British evacuate Boston in March 1776; how did she get there?

Enderby family correspondence in the British Library is curiously silent about Nathaniel and Mary, apart from a statement that they married and Mary returned to England in 1781 with two daughters, Mary and Elizabeth, and 14 The Grove, Blackheath was leased for her from the Morden College from whence the information came, and that the lease was renewed by Sam and a Mr. Larkin in 1800.

Part of the family papers is a misnamed 1874 letter known as "the nephews and nieces letter," which contains a lot of early information on the Enderby family, but nothing on the Wheatelys. The three Wheatley ladies are mentioned in wills, by their Wheatley names, indicating that none of the three married; the mother would be in her sixties and the daughters in their forties at the time of signing the wills in the 1820s. The fact that none married is curious as is why the brothers left them more money than anyone else apart from their wives.

The nephews and nieces letter is a good example of so called professional historians following one another and in one case of falsifying the wording in the letter to make things fit. The letter is anonymous, not signed by anyone nor is it addressed to anyone; it was found amongst the papers given to the Library by Mrs. Moffit's [Helen Gordon] and Mrs. Blunt's [Mary Gordon] wills in the 1930s. A phrase in the letter and in her will suggest that Mrs. Moffit wrote it herself.

Two passages in the letter say "your grandfather, my great-grandfather", the second says "my great-great-grandfather", so the letter has to be written by a younger generation to a person of an older generation.

If there had been no Boston Tea Party, there would have been no American War of Revolution, therefore no United States of America, and no First Fleet to Australia. When convicts could be no longer sent to America as cheap labour, they were eventually sent to Australia.

* * *

Nathaniel Wheatley is said by lazy American historians to have married in London and remained there, dying in 1783/1803. They have no evidence for this at all. They also libel him by calling him a Loyalist when he was a Patriot. Leaving Boston and Providence, R.I., when the British arrive and the loss of his ship *Hero* when on a voyage to America's ally France, does not sound like a Loyalist to me. Alexander Coffin was repatriated; he, along with his brother(?), are mentioned in Samuel Enderby II's December 1775 letter intercepted by the British Authorities, to Nathaniel in Providence, R.I., saying that they were in London undecided what to do. Was this a hint to Nathaniel?

THE HOLSWORTHY CONNECTION

Protestant Religion in the First Fleets To Australia.

Twice can be said to be a coincidence; three times means an outside reason. These three ladies, the most important in the first thirty years of Australia's modernisation, have a lot in common, which would appear to have gone unnoticed.

Prior to marriage, Mrs. MacArthur, Mrs. King and Mrs. Macquarie all lived in the same locality. Two of the couples married in the same church in the remote, rural, southwest of England in the headwaters of the River Tamar, a river that has been at the forefront of protestant religion, possibly commencing with Sir John Elliot, first elected to the British Parliament in 1614, knighted in 1618. His death through being imprisoned in the Tower of London in 1632 made him a martyr for the Protestant cause and the 1640 British Civil War; which was largely a war over religion. The Elliot's abode is at Port Elliot, Torpoint, Cornwall, south of Saltash.

Sir John Elliot was a supporter of the Massachusetts Bay Company, in which Evangelical Protestantism was one of the reasons for emigrating. The descendents of the original emigrants and financiers on both sides of the Atlantic assisted in organising the First Fleets to Australia, their momentum and ability to do so was drastically cut with the death of Pit the Younger, Prime Minister of Great Britain, in 1806.

The first European immigrants to Virginia were transported by private ships, one captain of which, Captain John Smith, says in his seventeenth-century book, *Generall Historie*, that the immigrants were assisted by a group of people: *"Some were gentlemen, some merchants, some handy craftsmen. These dwell most about London; they are not a corporation but knit together by a voluntary combination without constraint or penalty, aiming to do good and plant religion."*

It was Boston, Lincolnshire, merchants that helped the Pilgrim Fathers get out of jail and a ship to Holland, possibly indicating a larger organisation than that suggested by Captain Smith. As time went on, the voluntary combination had to have some organisation for control; I would suggest that in the latter part of the eighteenth century, Morden College, Greenwich, would have been a good candidate for this position, being an organisation and Protestant.

The Blackheath/Greenwich area was a noted area for religious dissention from the accepted Catholic religion, centuries before King Henry VIII instituted the Church of England at his palace in Greenwich, possibly starting with the slaughter of Alphege by invaders; he was quickly made a saint and the local church is named in his honour.

The Holsworthy Connection is evidence of this religious background to the First Fleets, as is the numerous [all?] subscribers to Phillip's book of his years as Australian Governor; many are well-known anti-Catholics, stringent Protestants, many of whom had a dwelling in Greenwich/Blackheath. Pitt the Younger and Lord Sydney had to pass through the Blackheath area to get to London.

Subscribers to Phillip's book did not have time to read it before being published. Phillip did not have time to write it between landing and publishing, so subscribers must have supported the book for some other reason. The £17,000 left by Phillip when he died and cannot be accounted for by a biographer may have been the subscriptions, approximately £37 per subscriber, or £12 per book, or a direct contribution from the whaling industry as can be inferred from sections of Enderby Captain Thomas Melvill's letter to his employers about his catching of the first Australian Whale and extracting oil from it.

The River Tamar came to the mind of more than one person upon their first sight of Sydney Cove. Saltash is an ancient town on the Cornish bank of the Tamar, home to sailor John Hawkins and his nephew Francis Drake, a little upstream from the new upstart of Plymouth [Saltash was a town when Plymouth was a sheepfold on the Down, is *a Cornish ditty*] and the castle of Lord Eliot at St. Germains, [the family of Sir John Elliot raised to the Earldom of St. Germains, the family being connected by marriage to that of the Prime Minister Pitt's and that of the Earl of Stanhope] and the Monarch's castle of Trematon [where Drake stashed his loot whilst he went to London to tell Queen Elizabeth I] on the River Lyhner, a tributary to the Tamar.

MRS. MACARTHUR

Elizabeth Veale, a lady who has been cheated out of her true recognition by Male Chauvinism, was born in England, at Holsworthy in the headwaters of the Tamar Valley, which separates the old counties of Devon and Cornwall for most of their common border. Had the river gone much further, it would have made Cornwall an island.

At the age of twenty, which, for the time, was old enough to be getting married, she married in a hurry to one John MacArthur, who had a commission in the Durham Light Infantry. In October 1789 Elizabeth Veale became Mrs. John MacArthur; they were married in St. Peter and St. Paul's church, Holsworthy, Devon, at which the bride's relatives are said to have soon noted the groom's haughty manner. Having been on half pay for six years, he swapped his commission from the Durham Light Infantry for one in the NSW Corps as soon as it was formed in June 1789. Why was he so keen to go to New South Wales? Why was he allowed to take his wife? Others were not.

How the courting of these three couples was accomplished puzzled me. The MacArthur courtship according to a neighbour, a descendant of the King clan, [at least one King married a MacArthur] was done during the six years on half pay when MacArthur resided for several periods in Holsworthy, enjoying the district's fox hunting on the lands of the Earl of Stanhope, [Phillip Stanhope the 4th Earl of Chesterfield. resided in Greenwich, a neighbour of the Enderbys as was the Earl of Sandwich who was the First Lord of the Admiralty] and courting at night.

Fourteen months later, the embarkation of the NSW Regiment having been delayed, Lieutenant MacArthur, wife, Elizabeth, and son, Edward, boarded the whaler *Neptune*, [owned by the Protestant family of Samuel Enderby II, spokesperson for the British whaling industry and trans-Atlantic shipping, also a supporter of the Massachusetts colony, his son Samuel III being a toast at the MBC 200th anniversary dinner] and set sail for Australia, but not before MacArthur duelled with the ship's captain John Gilbert, necessitating replacement by Donald Trail. Apparently, he did not like the accommodation assigned to him. He had another duel with the captain of his regiment by the name of Nepean, who had the family transferred to the *Scarborough* in mid Atlantic. Capt. Nepean is the brother of Under Secretary Evan Nepean who has a lot to do with the First Fleets and whaling. [*Both Nepeans came from Saltash. The author's two sons were baptised in the same St. Stephens by Saltash church as were the Nepean brothers.*] In Cape Town, MacArthur fell into the harbour whilst embarking in a ship. They eventually arrived in frontier Sydney in June 1790; the bride had been given a preview of what a part of her life was to be like. Some medical authorities hold that these and subsequent actions were due to his mental condition that he eventually died from in 1834; more like he was a bully boy with some ability, which enabled him to get away with it.

A year later, 1791, the MacArthurs transferred to Parramatta, He was given 100 acres of land that became Elizabeth Farm; having had a house built on the land, he was given another 100 acres. In 1793, MacArthur was appointed Inspector of Public Works. As well as his regular military duties, he was Paymaster for the NSW Regiment, so he would not have much time for the farm. Subsequent events would suggest that all agricultural work was the province of Elizabeth MacArthur, this intelligent, hard working mother of seven children, six being raised. Elizabeth MacArthur showed an aptitude for botany; in astronomy, she was tutored by Lt. William Dawes. Surgeon Worgon of the *Sirius,* taught her to play the only piano in the colony, which he left to her upon his leaving for England.

MacArthurs **did not** import the first Merino sheep; this was done by Captain Waterhouse RN, who was persuaded by Commander Gydley King RN to buy the Merino sheep from the widow of the Dutch Commandant of Cape Town, Captain Gordan, who had committed suicide at his defeat by the British. Waterhouse sold two rams and four ewes to the MacArthurs when he had to return to England in 1798. Commander King [later Gov. King] was probably informed, on his 1791 mystery London visit, of King George III's Merino sheep in Kew Park and of their potential to Great Britain, by Chief Shepherd Sir Joseph Banks.

John MacArthur was in England 1801 to June 1805, and again from 1809 to 1817. So it was impossible for him to have any influence on the sheep breeding, even if he did know the difference between a ewe and a ram. A letter taking six months in either direction could miss the breeding season. Being the son of a shopkeeper from Plympton, near Plymouth, in the army at fifteen, he would not be as familiar with sheep and animals as his wife was, she being a farmer's daughter. A farm in the Holsworthy area would probably be mainly sheep with a few cows. During the **eight year** stay in England, he was assisted in his troubles by Lord Camden, who was Pratt the lawyer before being raised to the peerage by "Pitt the Elder." This may be why the MacArthur homestead was called Camden.

From "The Four Georges" by J.H. Plumb: *"Once when Franklin* [Benjamin] *was talking to Pratt, the great lawyer, later Lord Camden and a friend of Chatham* (who was 'Pitt the Elder,' Prime Minister of Britain krd), *Pratt prophesied that with the conquest of Canada, the Americans would set up for independence. Franklin replied that no such idea had ever entered their heads, nor he said would it unless you grossly abuse them. Very true said Pratt that is one of the main causes I see will happen and it will produce the event."* An indication of a long term conspiracy? Lord Stanhope took Benjamin Franklyn the Massachusetts British Agent, to the House of Lords to hear the debate on the American Colonies.

Mrs. MacArthur was held in high esteem by all who came in contact with her; the following are things said of her at the time and show what kind of a person she was. It was Mrs. MacArthur who instigated the practice of grubbing out the tree roots to facilitate better cultivation. Bread was often in short supply in the early years. Guests when invited to dinner with the Governor, had to take their own bread, but not Elizabeth. Governor Phillip said there would always be bread at his table for her. An 1814 letter from Mrs. MacArthur to the United Kingdom survives. In it, she says: "*We grow wheat, barley and oats, we make hay, at least I do and so does Mrs. Macquarie, but the practice is not general. We feed hogs we have cattle, keep a dairy, fatten beef and mutton and export wool.*"

Gov. Macquarie gave *her a grant of 600 acres* of land near Elizabeth farm, "*as a mark of approbation of her exertions for the agricultural and rural improvement of the country.*"

John MacArthur did not claim the success of the sheep breeding for himself; it was thrust upon him by the male orientated society of the day. This is revealed in a letter he sent to Lord Bathurst, the Colonial Secretary: "*It was Mrs. Macarthur's able management of his flocks that had resulted in an improved breed of sheep and increased yields of wool.*" With MacArthur out of the country or doing his military duties, it was Elizabeth who instructed the workers—convicts and free, men and women—with just a shepherd to assist, with no recorded trouble at Elizabeth Farm.

John MacArthur is erroneously given credit for the Merino sheep, whilst nothing is said of his pioneering of the wine industry. During his stay in England, 1809-17, he and his three sons went to Europe during school holidays, learning about vines and wines. MacArthur imported many vines that he planted at Camden and Nepean, importing trained vine dressers to look after them. By 1827, the property was producing 100,000 litres of wine annually. His sons carried on the growing. Sir William MacArthur, his son, gained medals in Europe for his wine and brandy.

Mrs. MacArthur died at Clovelly [the name of a quaint

north Devonshire town in England not far from her birth-place], the home of her daughter and son-in-law, Mr. and Mrs. Henry Watson Parker [Government Private Secretary] on 9 February 1850, age eighty-one, never having left Australia once she set foot upon its soil. A granddaughter said of her: *"Through all the difficulties and trials that beset her path, her Christian spirit shines forth, and in all her letters to her children, with whom she corresponded regularly until her death, there is found no complaining or ill-natured word."* Elizabeth MacArthur lived in a harsh world, and worked in a masculine occupation in which she triumphed in a spectacular way, putting Australia well and truly on the map, so that when gold came along, the world knew where Australia was. She must have seen a huge difference in Sydney and surrounds by 1850.

MacArthur spelt his name in this fashion when he signed the writ of Rebellion.

To rectify their error in placing John MacArthur with a Merino sheep on a banknote, the Australian Federal Government and Reserve Bank should issue the next note with Elizabeth MacArthur's portrait and two Merino Sheep in a higher denomination than $2; $50 would not be too high.

Mrs. MacArthur is the Australian of the Millennium.

MRS. KING

The second lady of the trio is Anna Josepha Coombes, born a stone's throw away from Holsworthy at Hatherleigh, still in Devon. Miss Coombes would have attended the local church. When Lieutenant King arrived back in England from Australia, acting as a Postman, [why was it necessary for him to hand deliver these letters? Subsequent reports and letters were not] he delivered his letters, dashed off to Devon, found Anna, who was in her mid-twenties, living in Barnstaple not far from her birthplace, her parents having died; he gathered her skirts up and whisked her off to London where they were married in the relatively new church of St. Martins in the Fields, on March 11, 1791, shortly after Lt. King was promoted to Commodore .The fields have now become Trafalgar Square.

King told Anna, before the marriage, that he would probably have two children in Australia; after explaining the circumstances, she agreed to raise them as her own. I wonder if they realised their marriage date was the same date that the mother, Ann Innet, was sentenced to transportation? Ann gave birth to King's son, to be called, Norfolk, after his birthplace (Norfolk Island), and called the second son after his birthplace, Sydney. King no doubt introduced his wife [if she required introduction] to the whaling family of Enderby, suppliers of a large proportion of the ships for the early fleets, with whom he was very close. A lifelong family friend, he more than likely told them of his children at the same time. The illegitimate children of a convict, together with the legitimate children, stayed with the Enderby family when on holiday, whilst they were at school in England and later when they were in the Royal Navy. Norfolk became the first Australian born to be an officer in the Royal Navy.

Lt. Norfolk King was a POW in Virginia in the war between Britain and the United States in 1812, in which the British burnt down half-built Washington designed by a La Trobe, cousin or father of Melbourne's La Trobe.

The Enderbys lived in the very fashionable Greenwich, on the Thames River, on Crooms (Coombes, Cooms) Hill, or was this the gathering of likeminded people? In today's parlance, the Enderbys would be classed as millionaires. When Samuel Enderby II died in 1797, the Times newspaper called him a *"rich oil and St. Petersburg merchant."* Sam II is buried inside his local church, St. Alpheges, Greenwich, as is General Wolfe of Quebec fame.

Mrs. King started the first of three voyages to Australia in less than three months from being whisked off her feet. There is no record of any courtship in the King marriage. Gydley King being in the navy at the age of twelve, the only record of him having any leave is when his father died. Husband and wife in the three couples are said to be related, cousins or less. Courtship would be difficult because of the distance between the living places of the people concerned. Because of their religion and a relationship between each couple, I believe the marriages were arranged, but on amicable feelings between the partners.

Ann Inett had access to the boys; there is no evidence of any animosity between all concerned. Ann served her sentence, marrying convict Richard John Robinson on eighth of November 1792, who had accepted an offer by the Law of Britain to commute his death sentence to transportation to Australia for life. Governor King granted Robinson a free pardon in January 1804. They managed to own and run a hotel in Sydney, returning to her hometown of Droitwich, Worcester, England, in the 1820s.

MRS. MACQUARIE

Elizabeth Henrietta Campbell, of Airds, Scotland, was born a long way from Holsworthy; yet she and her husband Lachlan Macquarie, destined to be governor of Australia, were married, in a hurry, *in the same church as the MacArthurs*. Miss Campbell was staying with her society aunt in London, who was styled, Mrs. Campbell of Corwhin, probably to differentiate her from other numerous Campbells, when she first met Lachlan who was due to return to India.

Lachlan had made a vow when his first wife died in India that he would never take another wife to that country, so he asked her to wait for him till his tour of duty was done, which she did, rather reluctantly, as she was no longer a young miss; upon marriage she would be twenty-nine. In this marriage, we do have a record of a courtship, of a kind, as most was done by post, which in those days was not very speedy. Fortunately, most of the letters survive. From these we know that Elizabeth told Lachlan that she was going to live in Holsworthy, but not why; equally we know that Lachlan requested her not to go, but not why.

Lord Stanhope, a neighbour of the Enderbys and the Earl of Sandwich at Greenwich, had an estate there—actually he was the Lord of the Manor of Holsworthy. This would mean that he would have the control of the Living of the Church at

Holsworthy; he would be the main contributor to the vicar's wages and as such would have a large say in the vicar's appointment. Lord Stanhope took Benjamin Franklin to the House of Lords to hear the debate on the taxation of the New England colonies of North America.

There is an old saying that many a true word is spoken in jest. Was this being done in Lachlan's 1806 letter to Elizabeth, when he chides her about an *"old hoary lover"* whom he would *"call to account for making a conquest of her heart"*? He continued, the *"ancient rival must keep out of his way for safety's sake unless his beautiful daughter undertook to intercede for him."* Stanhope's attractive daughter, Lady Hester, was a "chip off the old block," for eccentricity. Was Lachlan meaning Lady Hester and Lord Stanhope? Lady Hester became virtually the ruler and religious leader of the western portion of Syria that now approximates to Lebanon, after the death of her bachelor uncle, "Pitt the Younger," for whom she kept house at 10 Downing Street whilst he was Prime Minister of Great Britain. Lady Hester is reputed to have committed suicide by sealing herself inside a crypt, by bricking the entrance up; at least, that is one of the stories about her death.

"Pitt the Younger" chose, with the assistance of the Evangelical and Ecclesiastical Societies such as the Clapham Sect, the Protestant representatives of the churches for Australia. Overseas clergy of the Church of England are supposed to be under the control of the Bishop of London; Australian early clergy never were.

Lachlan was supporting Elizabeth financially, unbeknown to her, through a third person. She was employed as the governess for the children of the Holsworthy vicar, who together with his wife, were the witnesses to her wedding.

Lachlan grabbed his opportunity to play postman when offered, the second postman in this trilogy to become Governor of Australia, which was an adventurous three-month overland trip from India to the Baltic, where he got a ship to Yarmouth, England, arriving on 17 October 1807. Quickly delivering the letters and doing his business, he dashed of to Devon with a fourteen-day marriage license from no less a personage than the Archbishop of Canterbury, the chief official of the Church of England, and on 3 November 1807 he had married Elizabeth, his half cousin, in the same St. Peter and Paul's church in which the MacArthurs were married. All six of these people can be said to be practicing Christians.

Holsworthy's church of St. Peter and St. Paul, is not the first church of that name in the story of Australian settlement by the British. St. Peter was a fisherman; St. Paul was a preacher. Liza Picard [a lady with a Mona Lisa smile and a sense of humour] in her book *Dr. Johnson's London*, quotes an almanac entitled *The Ladies' Complete Pocket Book*: "*The saints day for St. Peter and St. Paul is the 29th June; St. Peter and St. Paul were co-operators under our Saviour in the Conversion of the World.*" Viscount Sydney is buried at Seal, Chislehurst, Kent, in St. Peter's and Paul's. How significant is this combination, to America and Australia?

The three Holsworthy couples are not, by a long way, the only early settlers from the Tamar Valley. The MacArthurs, when entertaining certain people, had a toast: "**To the Banks of the Tamar.**"

The Two Postmen eventually became Governors of Australia!

Two of the three couples travel to Australia as Governors to be. [King and Macquarie]

Two of the ladies are buried in Australia. [MacArthur and King]

One lady travelled three times to Australia. [King]

One lady never left Australia having put her foot on its soil. [MacArthur] *Who said there was no Romance or Mystery in Australian History?*

The old rectory where Mrs. Macquarie lived is now the Museum for Holsworthy, which confirmed the above story.

LT. RALPH CLARK, MARINE, IN *FRIENDSHIP* OF THE FIRST FLEET

Lt. Ralph Clark, Marine, came from the Musselborough area of Durham in the north of England, so the following comments are not partisan. He did live in Plymouth with his wife, as that was the home port for the marines. He wrote the following upon entering Port Jackson for the first time; "*Blessed be to that we have got save to anchor in one of the finest harbours in the world. I never saw any like it. The River Thame is not be mentioned to it and that I thought was the finest in the world. This said port Jackson is the most beutifull place. I cannot compair any think to come nearer to it than about 3 miles above Saltash to the weir.*" Saltash is on the Cornish, Westerly bank, of the Tamar River. The Collins brothers are said to have lived in Saltash prior to founding Tasmania, taking quite a few Saltashians with them. The Nepean brothers were born in Saltash.

Evangelic Protestantism was one of the reasons for the colonisation of Australia; another was the oil industry of the day—whaling. The Indian and Pacific oceans were reported to be well blessed with the most lucrative whale, the spermaceti. Evidence of this, by East India Co. crews, is part of a government enquiry into whaling bonuses, which were paid for *another* eleven years from 1787 [1776+11=1787], 1776 being the year that Massachusetts ports were denied to the British Whaling Fleets; the bonuses, paid by the British Government, included bonuses of £800, £700 and £600 [at the time a whalers catch—not profit—did not average £4,000 for a three year cruise] for the first three ships to enter the Pacific Ocean via Cape Horn [Drakes and *Endeavours* route] and return with whale oil. Enderby ship *Emelia*, on her maiden voyage, rounded Cape Horn in 1788[!] returning to London with a full cargo too soon to qualify, having to wait downstream until she qualified. The ship was named for Emelia Vansittart. The second ship was also an Enderby ship—*Friendship*—captained by Thomas Melvill. This *Friendship* is not the First Fleet *Friendship* which sank on its way home. The name is more an indication of the owners' religion—the Society of Friends, otherwise known as Quakers. Enderby family papers say Sam II was a Quaker but the Society of Friends HQ in Leeds, Yorkshire, United Kingdom, have no record of them but would be pleased to accept them if proved.

Notes by the author, who worked for the Saltash Borough Council in the 1960s: Saltash is an ancient town on the west and Cornish bank of the river Tamar that separates the counties of Devon and Cornwall. The Tamar River goes from the south coast nearly to the north coast. It is a steep-sided river; in geographic terms it is a Ria, a drowned river valley, with deep waters which kept the Romans out of Cornwall whilst they occupied the rest of England and Wales and built a couple of walls to keep the marauding Scots out. Historians often say Plymouth instead of Saltash.

Francis Drake married Saltashian Mary Newman, who paid rates on a house in Fore Street, Saltash, a few doors down the street from the Guildhall. The council can exhibit the rate book, which also shows that Drake's uncle, John Hawkins, old sea dog, lived on the waterfront and also paid rates. It is possible the author assisted in removing the Hawkins residence whilst reconstructing the waterfront of its *picturesque slums* for habitable dwellings. The sixteenth-century rate book not being able to be translated to the twentieth-century buildings, it was difficult to establish which one was the Hawkins building. Quite a bit of unrecorded building on the only horizontal riverfront land took place in 400 years!

Lt. Clark is recorded as living with other marines in Plymouth; he was married to his beloved Alicia, of which his diary is full of lamentations that he has left her. Clark wished to bring his wife on the First Fleet but being on the bottom rung of the officer ladder prevented him from doing so, although sergeants could and MacArthur did.

Lt. Clark eventually returns to his beloved Alicia, but not before he has a daughter with convict Mary Branham on Norfolk Island, on 23/7/1791. The daughter was called Alicia—compliment or insult to the two adult females? On his return to Plymouth, he sees for the first time, Ralph Jr. The Clarks have some time together before Alicia dies in childbirth or shortly after. The two Ralphs are aboard the same Royal Navy ship *Sceptre* in the West Indies, when in the same week of June 1794, both die, one from yellow fever, the other falling from the mast; which died first and from what is not clear, possibly due to having the same name. Ralph Sr. at least left a useful personal diary of the First Fleet voyage and the early years of Sydney. He was in the ship *Friendship* and is credited with the phrase "The Fighting Five In Friendship" referring to five female convicts who he had put in leg irons because of their fighting friendship. His diary is a record by an ordinary person, as ordinary as any First Fleeter could be. Mary Branham, time served, with Alicia Branham and William Branham a Marines son, were all repatriated to England.

QUEEN OF THE HUNTER

In Diddlebury near Ludlow in county Shropshire
Rat Catcher Jones plied his trade for hire.
The last day of January seventeen hundred and sixty two
His daughter Mary was baptised with dew.
Known to all as Molly for most of her life
Jones changed to Morgan when William took her for his
                                                    wife.
In seventeen eighty nine Molly stole a hank of hempen
                                                    yarn.
At Shrewsbury Assizes the judge used Molly to warn
Sentencing her to seven years transportation
Did not improve her situation.
Leaving husband and two children in Diddlebury
Molly at 28 landed at Port Jackson in a hurry
From officer's quarters of *Neptune*
In seventeen ninety at the end of June.
For favours bestowed Molly lived outside the prison wall.
Always willing to work Molly soon walked tall.
September seventeen ninety one HMS Gorgon came to
                                                    port
Amongst the convicts put ashore William Morgan stood
                                                    fraught.

William arranged for children to be looked after by
another
He stole, gave himself up, was transported to be with their
mother.
The Morgans were not the only husband and wife team
to be sent.
Given the where-with-all to build a house all was happy
as meant.
Molly did not settle down, William cramped her style.
With two years to go, Molly used her charms to wile
American F. Locke on ship *Resolution* to make the most
Successful escape from Jail Australia he could boast.
Landing Molly and thirteen others at a place like
Axmouth Roman Harbour from there to hike.
Molly hiked west to the city of Exeter.
Where the children joined her.
Molly went her westerly way to Plymouth.
As a seamstress, she put food in their mouth.
Bigamously marrying prosperous Thomas Meares
All went well for a few years.
In eighteen hundred and three Molly torched
The Meares Brass Foundry without getting scorched.
What evidence to say Molly had done the deed
Magistrates of Croydon near London had no need
Mary Mears was sentenced a second time to the colonies.
Arrival on whaler *Experiment* welcomed by her cronies.
Ten years between arrival
Molly saw a difference to survival.
Old and trusted ways saw Molly outside the wall.

Molly had a life reappraisal, she again walked tall.
Molly acquired some of the world's wealth.
By 1809 working her own land showing good health.
In 1814 Molly's herd of cattle made tongues wag
Guilty of rustling a Government beast with tag
Molly's defence of payment for favours received
Made many wives believe they were deceived.
Molly was sent to the Hunter valley
Which appears to have been right up her alley.
Wallis Plains is where Molly came to reign
Soon to be known as Molly Morgan's Plain.
Molly became Queen of the Hunter by being industrious
Her land was tilled her vineyards prosperous
Her grog shanty euphemistically named, Angel Inn.
Molly had a sense of humour shown in
The name of the shanty and of her abode Greta
On Anvil Creek is awfully close to Gretna.
Where English runaway couples married in Scotland
Over the blacksmiths anvil in Gretna with a gold band
They did marry
Molly did not tarry
To Gov. Brisbane for mercy in hanging fruit stealers
Sentenced by Magistrate Mudie a murky dealer.
Molly earned her title Queen of the Hunter
By working for the society around her.
At Greta a bush hospital she ran
In establishing a school she was in the van.
A young soldier Thomas Hunt, and Molly in 1822 did
wed.

"Toy boys are not new" she said, on the way to the
                                            bigamous bed.
Gov. Brisbane gave a lease on 60 hectares of land
Gov. Darling converted to a grant in her hand.
Molly, encouraging Maitland development
Did not record land sales with the Government.
The land muddle took a while to sort.
Many people thought Molly a good sport.
William Morgan died 1828, in the town of Concord
Living with Eleanor Fraser, five children on record.
Molly died in 1835, aged seventy-three
Is buried beneath a Greta tree.
No known authentic picture of Molly exists.
Her attributes were not solely sexist.
If I were a betting man, she would have red hair.
For living life to the full she had the flair.
Molly a convict from a low birthright used what God
                                            gave her
She did no more than many who should have known
                                            better.

I visited the State School at Greta in the Hunter Valley in
June 2004. The school is near a stream known as Anvil Creek.
A school "house" is called Morgan, as is a local hill. Molly was
known in Greta, but my story was the first time the Head-
master had seen it all together. The school existing in 2004 is
not the same school building that Molly subscribed to.

THE RAT CATCHER'S DAUGHTER

This heroine may, by some standards, be judged not a lady, but she died a queen, a title given to her by her neighbours. By her own efforts, she had risen above her lowly birthright, that of a Rat Catcher's Daughter.

Before the days of combine harvesters, wheat and other cereals were harvested by hand reaping. A number of stalks were tied together with twine [string] forming a sheaf. The stalks were far longer than they are today and formed bedding for animals kept indoors during winter. The stalks were called straw. Even numbers of sheaves were lent against one another waiting to dry; these were called stooks and formed hiding places for children. When the sheaves were dry, they could be transported to the farm where they were to be stacked awaiting the threshing machine. The stacks of unthrashed cereals were a pantry of food for rats, mice and other vermin, the catching of which was done by the local rat catcher, who in Diddlebury, near Ludlow in the county of Shropshire, England, was called Jones.

Tom Jones and his wife, Margaret, were married in the spring of 1761, after the corn stacks had been thrashed and the new planting commenced, a slack period of employment for a rat catcher. On 31 January 1762, he and his wife had their baby daughter, Mary, baptised in the local church. Most of her life, she was to be known as Molly, but officialdom continued with Mary. Her mother, Margaret, would probably have to take credit for whatever rudimentary schooling Molly had, also for getting her apprenticed to a dressmaker. The apprenticeship may have been influenced by the father of Molly's illegitimate child.

Rats lived in close proximity to hay and straw stacks, which were so useful to those of amorous intentions. Molly's charms must have been considerable, as their power were to last her for more than seventy years. Such charms soon became noticeable to the local gentry, in spite of her lowly birth, which precluded her from any marriage stakes with the squires. Molly must have enjoyed herself as, for the time, she had reached the considerable spinsterish age of twenty-three when she married for the first and only legal marriage of her life. With at least one child to an unrecorded father, she married William Morgan, a carpenter and wheelwright from nearby Hopesay, on the twenty fifth of June 1785.

The latter half of the eighteenth century was a boom time in England. The Industrial Revolution was getting under way; new factories and towns were going up all over the country. The twentieth-century areas of intense activity—Liverpool, Manchester, Sheffield and Birmingham—had just commenced. The potteries of nearby Stoke, such as the famous works of Josiah Wedgwood, ensured prosperity in the region, sufficient to give two people with trade qualifications a reasonable standard of living. William had saved a bit of money sufficient for them to purchase a local cottage, and Molly's earnings from dressmaking and altering at home had enabled them to renovate the cottage to a comfortable standard. A second child for Molly had been born in 1786.

After four years of marriage, Molly stole a hank of hempen yarn, a material used in rope and canvas making. A poor cousin of the mulberry, it has a reputation for having weak narcotic properties when chewed. In its raw state, it is an inexpensive item, imported from the Baltic and Ireland. Molly was caught and sentenced to seven years transportation at Shrewsbury Assizes on August 8 1789.

Having left her two children and husband behind in England and having spent about six months on the hulk of a prison ship on the River Thames tidal flats, awaiting a ship to take her to Australia, Molly Morgan, at the age of 28 found herself stepping off *Neptune*, of the Second Fleet, at Port Jackson (Sydney), Australia, on 28 June 1790. Capt. Nepean and Lt. John MacArthur of the NSW Regiment and his wife and child were also aboard at the commencement. Molly's voyage had not been as onerous as for some. She had used her charms to her advantage; the rewards were easier living conditions offered by a ship's officer. I can imagine MacArthur not liking Molly's presence so close.

Repeating her tactics at the woman's prison in Parramatta, she soon had permission to live outside the prison, which of course gave her more freedom. Molly was doing quite well for herself, having been in Australia just over a year. Then on 29 September 1791, her husband stepped ashore from *HMS Gorgon* in Port Jackson, as a convict. William must have been very much in love with Molly, first to take her as his wife with her child, then after arranging with relatives to look after the two children, to deliberately steal something to get transported to be with Molly.

The authorities having found out that the two were indeed man and wife, reluctantly gave the couple the materials to build a dwelling, which would not have been difficult for William, a carpenter; he would have been a useful addition to the population. The reluctance was because it took the belle of the ball out of the party scene. Molly may have shown the party goers, if they had needed showing, a pleasurable way of using Norfolk Island hemp, which was derived from its native flax.

It would appear that William cramped Molly's style. She had not reached the stage in life where she would acquire some of the world's wealth. Molly must have gone back to her old habits of enjoyment without any care for the consequences. After barely four and a half years in Australia and more than five of her seven year sentence served, Molly used her charms on one Capt. F. Locke, an American, of the good ship *Resolution* to take her and thirteen others aboard and sail for England. This he did, on 9 November 1794, which is the most successful escape ever from "Jail Australia." All were landed in England. Why Molly and Locke did what they did, only they know. We must presume that living with her husband was not to her liking. Captain Locke fell for Molly's charms hook, line and sinker; he must have known what the result would be to his professional standing. He was an experienced captain; he had captained the British whaler *Neptune* in 1780 for the influential Enderby Company. All captains knew that they should see written permission for someone to leave Australia.

Locke would know that his ship sailing and fourteen convicts going missing at the same time would lead to the only conclusion that they were on board. Such a number could only mean that he knew and agreed to their being there. He would also know that he would not be allowed to hold a position aboard any British ship. As far as whalers go, British or American, he did not.

Capt. Locke proposed to Molly, who fended him off somehow and still persuaded him to put them ashore at some out-of-the-way place on the English south coast, such as the disused Roman harbour of Axmouth, Devon, the start of the Roman Road known as the Fosse Way, which ended at Lincoln. The illegal passengers could not be put ashore at a regular port as the authorities would be suspicious of such a large body of people arriving from Australia. Also, a faster ship may have reached England before them and told the story so that officials would be waiting for them,

From Axmouth, it would be relatively easy for Molly to get to Exeter, which was on the major coach roads to the north, and to London, for her to obtain her children, and then go west to the city and port of Plymouth, Devon, where she set herself up as a seamstress. Eventually she met and bigamously married Thomas Mears, a prosperous brass founder. This marriage and subsequent ones were bigamous because William Morgan lived until 1828.

Molly must have been happy for a while until something upset her to the extent that she burnt down the Mears property in 1803. What evidence there was to say that Molly did the deed, other than her running away, we do not know.

She was caught at Croydon near London; Molly Mears was sentenced to transportation to Australia for the second time on 10 October 1803.

Molly arrived in Sydney aboard the Enderby whaler *Experiment* on 24 June 1804 as Molly Mears. Molly, now forty-two years of age, was welcomed by the old hands that were left; her fate had been pondered upon many a time. Ten years between departure and arrival would show a big difference in the standard of living and organisation of Sydney. Molly was by this time a well versed prisoner in the ways and means to make life easier. She was again lodged in the woman's prison at Parramatta, where she used her charms to ensure her living outside the prison walls. Molly had decided that one Thomas Byrne was to be her ticket out, which soon eventuated. The improvements to living may have awakened Molly to the possibilities of the country and that its climate made it much more habitable than Britain. Molly had a mid-life reappraisal, for she started to acquire some of the world's goods and kept out of serious trouble.

It is nice to think that she talked with her husband and his partner, First Fleeter Eleanor Fraser nee Redchester, who by this time had four children, the first being born on 8 September 1797. They were settled and happy to be in Australia, living on her thirty acre land grant at Concord. Molly's only legal husband, William Morgan, died in 1828 and is buried at St. Luke's, Liverpool. Eleanor died 18 November 1840.

Molly must have decided to stay in Australia, as in later life had the means to go back to England as a free and wealthy person, but never did. By 1809, Mary [Molly] Morgan had some land which was being worked. She did not often go into Sydney, for when she was given a land lease, she was advertised for (as Mary Morgan) in the Sydney Gazette to go and collect her lease. By using Morgan, it shows that the authorities had twigged that Mears was Morgan. There is no record of any punishment for the escape.

By 1814, Molly had sufficient land to have a herd of cattle, large enough to cause tongues to wag, which caused officialdom to investigate the many different brands on the cattle, including the government brand. Molly was charged with stealing a cow from the government herd. Found guilty on 26 March 1814, she was sentenced to seven years hard labour. Her defence was that the cattle had been payment for favours received. Mischievous or not, this defence caused a lot of gossip and matrimonial trouble for some of the top families of Sydney.

Coal at the mouth of the River Hunter, north of Sydney, had been found when the area was being searched for runaway convicts. A penal settlement had been established, to mine the coal, one shipload being exported to India, the first of many such ships over the years. Tales of the beauty and potential for agriculture in the valley were circulating in Sydney. The only way to get to a penal settlement was as a convict or as a guard. Molly got herself sent to the Hunter valley, to a place officially known as Wallis Plains, shortly, by popular usage, to be known as Molly Morgan's Plains, and she to be known as the Queen of the Hunter.

So Molly became a pioneer of both Sydney and that part of the Hunter now known as Maitland. It was as if she had found her place in society at last. Molly was industrious, and one way or another, her land was worked and she prospered as the flow of population kept coming, in spite of what the government wished. Molly was one of the first to plant vines in the valley, and she had a grog shanty/pub with the name of Angel Inn. It would appear that Molly got on well with men, not just in the sexual sense. There was no such connotation attached to Gov. Brisbane (1821-25)—he was more interested in star gazing—but he did give Molly a lease on 159 acres of land, which Gov. Sir Ralph Darling converted to a grant in 1830. On the 5th day of March 1822, Molly, at the age of sixty, took one Thomas Hunt, a nineteen-year-old soldier from the Wallis Plains Garrison, to her bigamous bed.

Molly earned her title Queen of the Hunter by working for, and giving to, the society around her, trying to make things a little more comfortable. She is credited with running a bush hospital at her dwelling. It would not be a hospital that you would recognize as such today, but back then, just to lie between washed sheets, probably the first time in years, and to have someone clean and bandage a wound, would be very therapeutic. Upon at least one occasion, she is credited with riding night and day to see Gov. Brisbane for mercy upon convicts sentenced to hang for stealing fruit, by magistrate James Mudie, a man whose background does not bear too much investigation: Mudie by name and muddy by nature. Molly also helped to start a school by a donation equivalent to $200, a no mean sum in those days.

Her prosperity was such that she purchased further land, amongst which was 203 acres at Anvil Creek. Molly may have had a sense of humour. She called her farm Greta at least that is the spelling that has come down through the years; it is very close to Gretna and was situated on Anvil Creek. Gretna Green in Scotland, the first town over the border from Carlisle in England, was the place until the twenty-first century that runaway lovers could legally get married over the blacksmith's anvil without parental consent.

Molly retired to her farm at Greta where she died at age seventy-three on 27 June 1835. The Australian newspaper of 23 January 1828 named her as one of the largest landholders in the Valley. No known authentic picture exists of Molly, which is a pity. What were her charms? They must have been more than the usual feminine assets; they certainly lasted a long time, at a time when cosmetics were not common, plastic surgery unknown, and soap and water not always easy to come by.

Molly's record was spoilt somewhat, when she tried to "do the right thing" in splitting her land up to form what is now known as Maitland and not having the sales recorded in a legal manner. People encroached onto land they had not paid for, since nothing was written down. It took years and a lot of money to sort out.

In the nineteenth century, women were not in the forefront of things or commercially minded. Molly, a convict from a low birthright, used what God had given her. Considering the conditions prevailing at the time, who can point a finger at some of her questionable morals? She did more than many to earn the title, given to her by the inhabitants of the valley—Queen of the Hunter.

CHARLOTTE, BUCCANEER

Charlotte Badger worked in Axminster, Devon, at the mill making carpets. On her way to the Stockland Inn, at the bridge over the salmon stream that ran through the village, she demonstrated her newly acquired ability to write, by scratching her initials on the bridge parapet. She could not read the plaque on the bridge that said: *"anybody found defacing this bridge would be transported to the colonies for life.."* Scratching her initials was her limit. The magistrate gave her no remission in her sentence.

Her three years in NSW, a year on the hulks awaiting a ship plus the voyage out, had really shown her many things that she would not have seen in the little corner of the world in which she was born. The soldiers' and sailors' old saying that travel broadens the mind was certainly true for Charlotte. The voyage out to Australia, calling at Rio de Janeiro and Cape Town, had whetted her appetite for travel. Then all the new things in Sydney—its beautiful harbour, the smell of crumpled gum leaves, the sunshine—caused a stirring inside her that she must see more of the world. She confided her thoughts to her best friend, Sarah Barnes, who, to Charlottes surprise, was determined to go with her. A few days and nights were taken up with discussing how to do so.

The night they heard that two servants were required in

Hobart, Tasmania, Charlotte realized that their opportunity to escape from the system had arrived. Before breakfast of cold water and porridge, Charlotte told the gist of the plan to Sarah who agreed. So the two of them volunteered to go to Tasmania, much to the surprise of the jailer, but then volunteers should make better servants than directed convicts and it saved him trouble, so they were put down to go. Charlotte's plan was audacious and marked her for what she really was: an intelligent, able woman, as her life story illustrates.

How was a poor defenceless woman to capture and command a ship? By using Eve's tactics, as Eves have always done on poor susceptible Adams. Whilst awaiting the arrival of the Brig *Venus*, which had been seen off the Heads, Charlotte and Sarah used this time to hone their plans to perfection. Charlotte should have been a general in the army; she would not have lost America. Charlotte was to be the Eve. Sarah could join in to whatever degree she wished, just as long as things got merry; Charlotte had no doubt that Sarah would enjoy herself doing what she had to do. Eventually the brig *Venus* docked and was readied for the voyage to Hobart.

Charlotte had good looks and attributes that she was not opposed to using to her advantage. Charlotte decided that the Mate, John Kelly, was the man for the job. The next few days would put this Adam under the influence of Eve and on the path to the hanging tree. Two days after sailing south from Sydney, the ship called in at Twofold Bay. By this time, Charlotte had worked on Kelly to the extent that Kelly would open the rum store and broach a keg for himself and a friend to make a foursome with Charlotte and Sarah—no grass grew under her feet. With the captain ashore by the ship's boat, the foursome partied on to the extent that the captain was aboard before they knew of his return. Being caught red-handed turned out to be in the favour of Charlotte and Sarah, as the captain injudiciously told Kelly, as he had the four of them clapped in irons before a flogging, that on reaching Hobart he intended to have Kelly arrested for neglect of duties.

Either the captain was not very good with his navigation or he required a second opinion before entering the dangerous Bass Straight, and there was nobody aboard except the mate who could give the required assistance, for the Captain had to release Kelly from the leg irons to give this assistance. Charlotte worked fast; she pointed out to Kelly one or two home truths about his future in Port Arthur, since they were on the way to Tasmania, that his maritime career was finished, so why not grab what was going? After explaining how this could be achieved, the two sailors were in the piracy game.

Charlotte's scheme was for Kelly to secure the firearms and to release three convicts she nominated and to give them the firearms when they neared Tasmania. This he did, releasing Charlotte, Sarah, and his friend, from their leg irons at the same time. Charlotte immediately assumed the position of captain, as of right, nobody thinking otherwise. "*The seven Musketeers*," armed with the ship's pistols and rifles, overcame the crew.

Charlotte had the ship's boats lowered to the gunwale and forced, by show of arms, the crew and the rest of the convicts into the boats and cut them adrift, only after Charlotte showed her temperament and mental attitude by personally flogging the captain, on the deck, before all. Vengeance is sweet. Before setting course for New Zealand, *Venus* boarded another vessel, transferring arms and food. The two women took turns at the helm while the five men struggled with the ship across the Tasman Sea. In the Bay of Islands, New Zealand, the seven were befriended by a tribe of Maoris. After unloading the stores, *Venus* was scuttled and her people lived for some time in peace with the Maoris.

Charlotte and Kelly stayed in the islands for a few years, always afraid that a ship coming for water would find out who they were, as both realized that the long arm of the law would be searching for them. Eventually, the captain of a watering British man of war was curious enough about a white couple that did not contact the ship, even for conversation about the world they had apparently left. By bribing some natives, he confirmed his suspicions and arrested Kelly, leaving Charlotte behind, as she could not be found. Kelly did not offer help to find her, as he knew that he would be the one in trouble with the law, being the ship's mate, having talked about the situation many times before; he knew that Charlotte would prefer to stay behind. When Kelly stood trial, the original captain was produced as a willing witness; he swallowed his pride and told of Charlotte's part in the happenings and of being flogged by a woman. John Kelly was found guilty for having failed to discharge his duties. His punishment was hanging from the gallows.

One day, *Lafayette*, on voyage from San Francisco to Newcastle, a place that did not exist when Charlotte left Australia, called at Vavau in the Tonga group of islands for water. The captain was surprised to be addressed by a white woman with a boy by her side. Charlotte must have been in a melancholy mood; the result was that she told the captain her full story. He was soon smitten with her still pleasant looks and demeanour and she sailed away with him to Newcastle.

Charlotte had been sold/exchanged/gifted by the natives of the Bay of Islands to a neighbouring chief, in this manner, possibly encouraged by Charlotte herself, being the adventurous spirit she was and to cover her tracks, should the British Law come looking for her, had arrived in the Tonga's. The boy was her son by the local chief, because his father was the Chief, he would not be allowed to go with his mother so she slipped quietly aboard, when *Lafayette* sailed. Charlotte was on her way back to Australia after a twelve year absence.

CHARLOTTE THE EXPLORER

Charlotte's life of adventure was not over yet by a long way; being born the same year as the First Fleet, she was around thirty five years of age when she alighted in Australia for the second time. The whole area was bustling with energy and prosperity; the controls on immigration into the Hunter Valley area had been lifted, not that they had stopped many determined people from settling in the pleasant, well-watered fertile valley. Investigating the prospects, Charlotte made the acquaintance of Molly Morgan, who was so popular that the correct name for the area, Wallis Plains, had been abandoned by the locals who called it *Molly Morgan's Plains* and she herself was referred to as *Queen of the Hunter.* Molly and Charlotte got on well with each other to the extent that she missed the sailing of *Lafayette,* if she had ever intended to leave on her. Molly gave her a job in her Angel Inn where she soon proved to be an asset. After a while, Charlotte could feel things stirring inside her; she was afflicted with wanderlust, which had not been quenched.

The barroom talk was all about the feller Cunningham who had found a pass in the Dividing Range up near Brisbane; he was the same feller that found Pandora's pass at the head of the Hunter Valley. It would seem that the escarpment that could be seen west of Sydney ran past Brisbane. If you did not get on top of the escarpment, you could perhaps never get off the coastal plain, which you had to do to get to China, for if you walked northwest from Sydney, you would eventually arrive there.

Charlotte made up her mind that she was going to China; to this end she made her plans over the coming months. The first decision was that preparations had to be made and that the best time to leave was the beginning of summer. The weather was warmer and by the time she got to the Brisbane area, it would be cooling down. The wet season they had up there would have filled the water holes, making travel easier.

Charlotte decided that she should obtain a horse. Obtain disguised the fact that she would have to steal one. There were other things she would need for such a journey: a hand axe, knife, spoon, bag, preferably of leather as a sack would not stand the usage such a journey would cause it, and a pot to boil things in. These were the bare essentials, she thought, and she would have to have time to obtain them. Due to this cautious planning, Charlotte managed all, including a pony and bridle but not a saddle, which was an expensive item. She set off one bright, moonlit night, being miles away by the time the owners had found their loss and reported it to the police. Nobody had lost a lot, the horse being the most expensive loss, so no one searched for Charlotte themselves. Consequently, the police did not bestir themselves overmuch either. Molly had told her that it could be better to go by way of the valley to her right at the junction of a tributary four days ride up the Hunter; this she did. She was now in virtually unexplored land, uninhabited by white people; the natives could be a real danger. She saw very few; the seasons had been good, plenty of waterholes, no need to gather around a few. Charlotte travelled through a succession of valleys steadily climbing higher until the summer days were very pleasant, temperature-wise, due to the altitude. Grass and water had been no problem. Her horse, not the youngest of animals, was feeling its age at the altitude. Nights were cold with very little shelter. Charlotte and animal were pleased when the going was downhill again.

She rode daily to a high spot on the escarpment edge overlooking a 2,000 foot drop, [600 metres] mainly to see where to head for next, but never got tired of the view around her. Still, she saw no natives. She did not realise until later that this could be from her travelling close to the edge of the escarpment. The natives had no need to go there; more food existed away from the edge. The open spaces and green grass, especially where the grass was recovering from having been burnt, reminded her more and more of her native England. It was in one of these day-dreaming spells that her horse surprised a black snake, which bit the horse on the foot. In the shemozzle that followed, Charlotte fell off her horse, nearly onto the snake. Fortunately, the snake slithered away, Charlotte picked herself up and gathered most of her belongings, which had scattered. Not all, however—a broken kitchen knife lay unseen in the bush.

Charlotte, after her fall, was shaken and walked with her horse along the edge of the divide. She noticed her horse was sick and realised that the snake had bitten the horse and it would probably be fatal. Charlotte camped early that night at the head of a small valley looking westwards towards the setting sun; there the horse died during the night.

Charlotte was now on her own two feet. What could she carry—what was needed? The axe was a must, for defence if nothing else; firewood was all around her. The pot was needed for cooking. Her flint tin was a must; it would last a while longer yet. Charlotte sat that morning and had a good think about where she was going. The escarpment was well defined here and to the northwest, she could see some hills. Determined to go on, she made for the hills. On her first day afoot, she came upon some natives, who were not hostile but wary of something they had not seen before. This encounter proved to be the same for all her encounters with the natives. She had to keep a close watch on her flint tin and axe once she had shown them their usefulness. Their fingers were as sticky as hers had been in acquiring them in the first place. By staying with the hospitable natives, she learned what, how, and where food was to be obtained. Having companions, after being so long on her own, was very nice.

One day, in a grassy, undulating plain, she came across a friendly tribe of natives comprising a whole range of ages from babies to old folk. It was a long time since Charlotte had been in a family situation and it was to her liking. One native man had a particular attraction for her, and the longer she stayed, the more they came together. None of the native females disputed their right to be together, so the first child was born in due course, followed by three more in time. Charlotte did not like constantly moving. It was all right when everyone could fend for themselves and travelled light, but she had been caught up in the age-old state of affairs that was not new to anybody, except Charlotte, the family situation.

The area in which she was living was open country, open to the winds that can blow cold; Charlotte told them about a shed and that they could make a large shed for protection of the whole tribe. This they did, using the axe to cut and shape the timber. Charlotte directed the construction of a European barn.

Whatever the colour of a person's skin and how well the people get on together, confine them within four walls and things start to happen. The squabbling and falling out made Charlotte realise that she would never get to China with the family tagging along, so one night, taking her axe with her, she set off along the valley to continue her journey to who knows where.

Charlotte's piracy *is true as far as we know the facts; she did arrive in Newcastle. Molly Morgan, Queen of the Hunter, did exist; the meeting of the two ladies is the author's imagination.*

Charlotte's explorer story is fiction to tie in the following historical facts.

Australian convicts often thought they could walk to China; many tried, none succeeded.

The second known European party on the Darling Downs area was Arthur Hodgson, a few months behind the Leslies who stayed in the Warwick area, whilst Hodgson went further north to the locality of present day Toowoomba. Hodgson, when looking for his land to squat upon, came across a group of natives that ran away leaving their belongings behind them. Hodgson, curious as to what their belongings consisted of, found that amongst them was a broken kitchen knife, upon the hasp of which was the maker's name and place of manufacture, which was Hodgson's old school town of Eton, after which he called his squattocracy, Etonvale. [When the squattocracies were being broken up for closer settlement, his nearest neighbour said "if you can call yours Eton, I am going to call mine Harrow," after the two Public schools in England. Another said, "you call these farms, stations, so I am going to call mine after a proper station," which he did, Euston station in London. These three places still retain these names.] Hodgson, when looking around the boundaries of his land, came upon a bleached skeleton of a horse in a valley head, near where Lt. Gorman's Irish jaunting cart was to come up the escarpment, as the first wheeled vehicle to do so, shortly after. This information is from Henry Stuart Russell's book "Genesis of Queensland" himself a contemporary of Hodgson and an early squatter at Cecil Plains near Toowoomba. He was often host to:

Ludwig Leichhardt, who states in his journal of his first and only successful expedition in 1843-44, that just east of present day Springsure in Queensland, he came across a small party of natives, amongst whom were three or four fair-skinned and blond-haired children, ranging in age from three to early teens. Leichhardt named the place Albino Downs; it keeps the name today.

Nearer to Springsure, a few days later, Leichhardt came across a portal frame of a hut, the wood obviously having been cut with an axe. Since the natives were known not to have metal, a European had been there before him. For this reason Leichhardt never claimed to be the first in that area.

The plaque on the bridge at Stockland was there in 1972 with many initials scratched in the parapet, mine included. They did serve a good pint of Flowers Keg at the Pub up the road.

EMELIA VANSITTART

Not a lady I would expect you to have heard of, Emelia
Vansittart never left Britain but was in the back seats of the
organising committee for colonising Australia. During the
relevant time, Emelia lived at 60 Crooms Hill, Blackheath,
Kent, England—the same road that Earl Chesterfield, the
Enderbys, and the Earl of Sandwich lived in. She had been
widowed in 1770 when her husband, Henry Vansittart Sr. was
aboard the ship *Aurora* bound for India when it left Cape
Town never to be seen again. Henry was to take up his second
appointment as supervisor for the East India Company.

Henry's father, Arthur Vansittart, had died in 1760, leaving
Henry and his brothers, Arthur, Robert and George, wealthy;
their grandfather, Sir Peter Vansittart, having died in 1705
leaving in excess of £100,000.

Widowed, Emelia was left to bring up the children: Henry
[Admiral], Arthur, Robert, George, Nicholas [Baron Bexley,
1766-1851] Emelia and Sophie. Henry became an Admiral, also
organised the building of the Enderby wharf at Greenwich.
Nicholas became Chancellor of the Exchequer for twelve years
under various governments.

Emelia Vansittart [1738-1818], a long-term investor in
Enderby Whaling, gave her name *Emelia* to the new ship that
was the first legal commercial ship around Cape Horn, to

obtain whale oil in the Pacific, return to London and claim the £800 bonus from the British Government, passing Cape Horn in the significant year of 1788. *Emelia* did the round trip in record time, arriving back in London too soon to claim the bonus, having to wait downstream. The speed of the voyage caused comment. *Emelia* was late leaving due to being on her maiden voyage. This construction delay could have been the reason for the First Fleet delay, *Emelia* having to rendezvous with the twelfth ship of the First Fleet, which would have been fishing in the Pacific, and transferred her cargo to *Emelia*.

Sophia Vansittart ran The Blue Coat School in Greenwich, she and the school being remembered in Enderby wills. It was probably the school Anna Maria King attended whilst living with Mr. and Mrs. Charles Enderby I and before marrying Hannibal Hawkins MacArthur.

MRS. JAMES COOK

Elizabeth Batts of the Parish of Barking married James Cook, parish of St. Paul, Shadwell, in St. Margaret's, Barking, on 21 December 1762, by special license from the Archbishop of Canterbury; this meant that they did not have to have the banns read at church for three Sundays prior to the marriage ceremony. They got married in a hurry. Mrs. Cook's mother was Mrs. Mary Batts. Before marriage to Samuel Batts, she was Elizabeth Smith, daughter of Bermondsey Currier, Charles Smith I. A currier is one who cures leather.

Samuel Batts died before July 1742 when his will was proved, leaving Mary Batts, widow, at least nine properties, and leaving four pounds per year to Samuel Batt's daughter, Sarah Ford, suggesting that Samuel Batts had been married before and that this daughter was married. There is a district to the east of Mile End, where Mr. and Mrs. James Cook lived, called Ford. Samuel Batts in his will, describes himself as a Victualler, which is different to what I was told at school, which was that they were poor and Mr. Betts was a Lighterman. Widowed Mrs. Batts marries John Blackburn of Shadwell. A John Blackburn, M.P. was a subscriber to Australian Governor Phillips Book.

Mrs. Batts nee Smith's, brother, Charles Smith II, a shipping agent of the Custom House, had a son Charles Smith III, a wholesale watchmaker of Bunhill Row, and a naval son Isaac

Smith. Therefore brothers Charles III and Isaac are nephews of Mrs. Cook. A Charles Smith assisted in the formation of the Bank of England. Charles III wife's name was Frances. They lived at Brunswick Place, Bowyar Lane, Lambeth, with their children: (Mary) Mariana Ellen, Charles James, and Frances. On becoming a widow, Frances Sr. became Mrs. Walford of Wateringbury, Maidstone, Kent. A Charles Smith was a Shipping Agent living at New Grove, Mile End, where the Cooks lived.

Isaac sailed with James Cook aboard *Endeavour* and is reputed to be the first to set foot on the Australian east coast. Isaac continued in the navy, retiring as an Admiral. After James Cook's death, Isaac lived with his aunt, Mrs. James Cook whenever he was ashore. Upon his retirement, they lived in her house in Clapham, London, until his brother, Charles Smith III, left Merton Abbey Gatehouse, near the Wimbledon Tennis courts to Isaac in his will. Merton Abbey is the founder of Merton College at Oxford. The gatehouse is a fitting abode for England's hero Lord Nelson to live with his lover, Lady Emma Hamilton, whilst she is a "lady in waiting" with their daughter Horatia. When Isaac died he willed the gatehouse to Mrs. Cook; when she died in 1835, the house no doubt formed part of the £60,000 she left, which is multi-millionaire money today.

THE GORDONS

The following is from the so called *Nephews and Nieces letter*, in the Moffit and Bell collection in the British Library. (They were both granddaughters of Samuel Enderby III and sisters of General Gordon of Khartoum.) The letter is about the Enderby family. It is an anonymous letter found in the papers of Samuel Enderby III's granddaughter, Mrs. Moffitt nee Helen Clark Gordon. Because a passage in Mrs. Moffit's will being very similar to one in this letter, I believe it to have been written by her (Helen Clark Gordon). Helen married her brother's medical colleague of the Chinese Opium Wars.

"The first three on the list were tanners at Bermondsey (London KRD), *I suppose of some consequence, as they appear to have had country houses away from the seat of business which was not customary then with small traders, as I find their residences to have been at Staines, Richmond, Kingston and Walthamstowe."* Being in the leather industry before whaling, the Enderbys could easily have known Mrs. Cook's grandfather, Charles Smith I, being in the same business and both being in Bermondsey, the centre of the British leather industry.

As whalers and shippers, they would know, or at least heard of, Charles Smith II, shipping agent at the Customs House, which was just downstream of the Enderbys at Paul's Wharfe.

Samuel Enderby II lived in Earl St. North London, not far from Bunhill Row where Charles Smith III had his clock/watch-making business.

Letters to and from the Enderbys mention a Cook of the Navy. Who this Cook is, is the mystery. What follows is what we know of who it can be. Captain James Cook, explorer, had a son also officially named James Cook who rose to be a commander before being accidentally killed or murdered in 1794, being found on a beach on the Isle of Wight, United Kingdom, with his head bashed in and his pockets turned inside out. This was after leaving Poole, Dorset, United Kingdom, where he had been when receiving a message from the Navy to get back to his ship in Portsmouth to take it to sea; he left Poole in a hired boat and crew. Why would he go to Poole if there was a chance his ship would be required to go to sea?

A letter from Phillip Gydley King from Norfolk Island to Samuel Enderby III, dated 20 July 1794, says: *"I see Jack Cook is a Captain; he is a worthy fellow but do not tell him so, he has used me ill, in not writing to me."*

A letter to Phillip Parker King from Samuel Enderby III, whilst King is Surveying Cape Horn, in a letter dated 19 November 1827 from London says: *"I have not seen Lieut. Cooke. I am told he is in Devonshire."*

The mystery deepens. Two Cooks are known to two generations of Enderby and King. The letters are 33 years apart. Did James Cook II have a wife and child in Poole that are unknown to history? Cook must have had a reason to go to Poole, no small distance from Portsmouth, when he was in command of a ship. Daniel Enderby II born 1681, died 1766, married Mary Cook, the mother of Samuel Enderby II.

Excerpt from C. Macarthur's letter to Phillip Parker King, whilst he is surveying Cape Horn [1828]: *"I could not have imagined Mrs. Cooke looking so blooming as she—for her appearance used to the delicacies; she is a good—and I think your gallant friend has made a happy choice. I met Mrs. Lethbridge, from . . ."* I am afraid C. MacArthur was not clear in his writing.

James Cook's grandfather lived in Roxburghshire in Southern Scotland. Why did he come south, the same as the MacArthurs, Campbells and Gordons? Were all taking the advice of Rev. Slaughter Clarke [great-grandfather of Gordon of Khartoum] of Hexam, Northumberland? This Reverend is reputed to have visited the South West of England several times a year. Hexam is a long horse ride from Devon, but it is convenient to Scots coming south of the border. Hexam is also the abode of descendents of the Samuel Enderbys and the descendents of Under-Secretary Evan Nepean.

The First Lord of the Admiralty is making enquiries as to who the Cooks mentioned are—no information to date.

Was James Cook a distant relation of the Enderbys? Cook had Slaughter relations in South Shields not far from Hexham. James Cook used "Young Slaughters Coffee House" in St. Martins Lane, London, whenever he was ashore.

Samuel Enderby II lived in Earl St. prior to 1783, not far from the Non-Conformist Cemetery near the Artillery Ground, where the first recorded game of cricket took place in 1744 and one side of which is Bunhill Row, where Charles Smith III made watches and or lived.

The Ladies of Darkie Gardiner

The first lady in his life was of course his mother who gave him his slight colouring. His mother was Annie Clark, with whom his father, Charles Christie, cohabited during the three years or so that he preceded his wife on Australian soil. A name like Annie Clark would suggest that she was not a full blooded Aborigine.

Frank (Francis?) Christie was born in 1830 at Boro Creek, near Goulburn. Such a situation was not unusual, the standard having been set by the First Fleets. Mrs. Christie arrived in Australia in 1832; she accepted Frank and brought him up with his three half sisters, who it is believed were the first to call him Darkie, which he did not seem to like. No doubt his sisters teased him all the more. It is supposed that the name calling was the reason why he ran away at the age of ten, to live with some Aborigines. At the age of thirteen, he was found working on a farm; he went back to live with his family for a while. By their later actions, his three sisters must have been particularly contrite about what their actions had caused Frank to do. Not all was their fault as he was a bit of a tearaway in his teens, just keeping beyond the long arm of the law, until he teamed up with Jack Newton.

In 1850, twenty-year-old Gardiner, alias Christie, along with Jack Newton and Bill Fogg were caught stealing horses, near

Geelong, Victoria, for which they received five years hard labour. Gardiner escaped from Pentridge prison on 26 March 1851.

Three years later, he was caught again for the same kind of offence and given fourteen years at Goulburn. After serving part of his sentence on Cockatoo Island, Port Jackson, Sydney, he was given a ticket of leave on 31 December 1859. Using the name of Clark, his mother's maiden name, twenty-nine-year-old Christie took up butchering, the ticket of leave being for the Carcoar area, from which he was absent at the time of cattle rustling; his ticket of leave was cancelled on 5 May 1861.

Gold Fever caught up with Frank, now using the name of Gardiner, which he may have got from his time in Melbourne (Port Phillip), as the present-day suburb of Malvern was originally called Gardiner, after John Gardiner, who was the original person to overland cattle south of the River Murray, and settled on the Yarra.

After unsuccessfully trying his luck on the Kiandra Gold Field, Darkie Gardiner joined up with a kindred soul and another ticket of leave man, John Presley. The two of them "bailed up" in the fashion of English highwaymen, on the roads of Bathurst and Lambing Flat gold fields, also around Yass, and probably on the turf of Australia's Capitol, Canberra. Presley separated from Gardiner and was caught and hanged on 23 March 1862. Darkie Gardiner then established a regular gang with Canadian Johnny Gilbert, who was shot by the police on 13 May 1865.

Gardiner in 1861 was in the Abercrombie Hills with a price on his head, £500. On 15 July of that year, the police were informed that Gardiner was at Fogg's house. Sgt. John Middleton and Trooper Hosie set out to capture Gardiner. On the sixteenth, they had Gardiner bailed up in Fogg's house. Shots were fired; Middleton was wounded twice. Hosie and Gardiner fired at each other, both receiving skull wounds and concussions. Upon coming round, Hosie set about Gardiner with his whip handle, on seeing Middleton being throttled. Gardiner was subdued and handcuffed; all was watched by the Foggs and their three children. Somehow, before Gardiner could be taken to the police station, he escaped, the how and the wherefore of his escape have never been satisfactorily explained. Middleton received a silver medal for bravery.

Gardiner, thinking it would be best to leave the district for a while, went to South Australia. On the way, he met up with Ben Holland, John McGuire, and Katie Brown, whom he knew from his "legal butchering" days. Their friendship blossomed, and he promised to return and take her away from the place and the man she was living with. The following year, 1862, he was back in the Abercrombie's, gathering a gang and planning "the big one," which was to be the gold coach that left Forbes every Saturday at four o'clock.

Trooper Pottinger's father had just died, the news of which reached Australia just before he was promoted to inspector, much to his disgust, feigned or real. The promotion was advertised with his correct title, that of Sir Frederick Pottinger, Inspector of Police, who vowed that he would clear up bushranging.

Gardiner teamed up with Ben Hall, [bushranger, shot thirty-four times, 5 May 1865] and six others: John Gilbert, Daniel

Charters, who afterwards turned informer, John Bow, execution commuted to hard labour for life, Alexander Fordyce, execution commuted to hard labour for life, Henry Manns, executed 26 March 1863 and O'Mealley, shot dead by David Campbell J.P. 20 November 1863. They all met in the Wheogo scrub outside Forbes, New South Wales.

The day they chose was 15 June 1862. The well armed gang awaited the coach about fifty kilometres along the road to Orange. Just before the time for the coach to appear, there came, fortuitously, two bullock carts, which were staged to appear bogged, causing the coach to slow down, along with its armed escort, enabling the coach to be easily robbed. When shots were fired wounding two guards, the horses bolted turning the coach over. The gold and money boxes were rescued.

Twelve policemen, led by Sir Frederick Pottinger arrived on the site the following Monday. Heavy rain that day made trackers useless. Working on the saying "once a thief, always a thief," Sir Frederick rode towards Ben Hall's place, arriving in the vicinity at the right time to see gang member Charters riding towards Hall's farm to collect saddle bags for Gardiner's share of the loot. Charters lost his nerve or sense and made a bolt straight back to the hideaway in the Wheogo, followed by Sir Frederick and his merry men. From the hideaway, Gardiner saw what was happening and was long gone by the time Sir Frederick got there, and had time to lay a diversion for the trackers, in that they sent a pack horse off in one direction and they in another, trackers fortunately following the pack horse. Since Gardiner did not have saddlebags, he would have hidden the heavy part of his share and kept the lighter folding money. The coach carried 5,509 ounces of gold and £7,490 in notes. The police recovered 20 percent of the gold and £135!

Gardiner kept his promise to Katie Brown, riding down for her on his black horse. The pair rode north to the vast and fast developing Queensland. Rockhampton had just had its farcical Canoona gold rush that never was and was preparing to receive the copper and gold ingots from Claramont to the northwest. Population was sparse; hence amenities were few and far between, with some of the metal going the shorter route to St Lawrence. When the Gardiners reached Rockhampton, they decided they had travelled far enough and that the ever increasing population would give them some protection; actually it played against them. The Gardiners had decided to set themselves up in business, and when they met up with the Craigs with similar ideas, it was natural for them to establish themselves in the same locality for mutual protection and society. They chose Apis Creek on the Rockhampton-Claramont track, the Gardiners running a general store and the Craigs having a Public house. Being two energetic couples in a sparsely populated district but on a heavily trafficked road, they soon made a go of their ventures. However, one day, Katie was feeling homesick, wrote to a friend to tell her sister where they were and how to get in touch with them. The "friend" got drunk and bragged about knowing where Gardiner was; the police got to hear of the braggart's claim and soon elicited the information.

All was going well for the foursome until March 1864 when all were arrested by a Lt. Brown of the Queensland police.

NSW police applied for extradition of Gardiner alias Christie, when they appeared before the Rockhampton Magistrates. At these proceedings, the Craigs were able to prove they did not know that Gardiner was Christie, a wanted criminal. This being supported by both Gardiners, charges of harbouring were dropped. Mrs. Gardiner claimed she was just living with her husband, although no marriage certificate was produced or asked for. Extradition for Gardiner to NSW was granted. Believing that some attempt could be made on the long land route to Sydney to rescue Gardiner, he was transported at the last minute by ship. This caught Katie on the hop and was not in Sydney for the first court appearance. Katie teamed up with Christie's half sisters to provide legal representation.

Sir Frederick Pottinger, Inspector of Police, could not find anybody, two years after the deed, who could remember sufficient to bring Gardiner to trial on the robbery of the Forbes coach; he was charged with intent to kill and murder John Middleton. Gardiner's barrister, arranged and paid for by the four women, defended Gardiner/Christie so well that the jury bought a verdict in of "Not Guilty"!

Gardiner was then charged with attempting to murder Trooper Hosie and wounding with intent to do grievous bodily harm. The four women in Christie's life yet again raised enough money to engage the successful barrister. This time, he was not able to get Christie off; he was found guilty of the non-hanging offence of intent to do grievous bodily harm. Other charges were brought against Christie. He had held up a Mr. Horsington and Mr. Hewitt on the Big Wombat Road near Young in March 1862. Horsington knew Christie from when he worked for Mr. Fogg, hence his testimony was believed. Christie pleaded guilty before Judge Sir Alfred Stephen on 8 July 1864 to the charges and received fifteen years hard labor for intent to do grievous bodily harm to Trooper Hosie. For armed robbery of Horsington and Hewitt, ten and seven years hard labor to run consecutively—thirty-two years total. Considering that one of the gang that he was the leader of had already been hanged for the robbery of the Forbes coach, and two received hard labor for life, he can be considered to have gotten off lightly.

The ladies continued the legal battle for years, with appeals and appealing to the Governors for clemency. It would appear that officialdom was getting a bit fed up with the ladies, and by the time that Christie had served eight years of his thirty-two and had been a model prisoner, the Governor of the day, Sir Hercules Robinson, amidst controversy and against the advice of the presiding judge, Sir Alfred Stephens, pardoned Christie, to be released in two years time, on the condition that he leave the colony. The pardon was effective on 20 July 1874; forty-four year old Christie sailed from Newcastle on the twenty-seventh for China.

All's well that ends well? This depends upon your point of view. One unfortunate happening was that just before the Governor agreed to the deal and transportation, Katie Brown went to New Zealand, to the Thames gold rush, to earn money quickly to continue the legal fight. For some reason, she committed suicide before the news of the Governor's deal reached her. How a woman was to make money quickly on a gold field, I will leave to your imagination. There was not a lot of easy money on this field and Katie did not leave much behind her. Christie must be the only native-born son of Australia to be *transported for life from Australia*. The legalities of the deal are questionable, but were probably welcomed by Christie and his sisters.

Christie did not stay in China, if in fact he got off the ship. The next we know is that he was married and keeping a pub/hotel on the San Francisco waterfront in the United States called *The Twilight Star*. There is a story of him having a shootout in the bar and killing a customer. Christie, using an alias of Frank Smith, finally died in the mid 1890s, as far as is known.

When I was showing off my local history knowledge around a Central Queensland campfire not far from Apis Creek, I was told the story did not end there. Twin grandsons are supposed to have visited, after their World War II service, the sites of their grandfather's exploits at Forbes and Apis Creek and went home with a big smile on their faces.

SEA KING BIRTHS

When Mr. and Mrs. Cmdr. P.G. King were going home to England from Australia in 1797 aboard an Enderby whaler *Brittannia*, the family changed ships at Cape Town for the extra room provided by the East Indiaman *Contractor*. Whaler accommodation was a bit cramped for the very pregnant Mrs. King who gave birth to daughter Elizabeth on 10 February 1797, before the ship reached St. Helena Island in the Southern Atlantic, which was to become the home for Napoleon.

Lt. King, as he was in 1790 on his mysterious visit to London, acting as a postman, saw King George III's Merino sheep in Kew Park, London, and the importance of the sheep was explained to him by the chief shepherd, Sir Joseph Banks. On this 1797 trip, before leaving Cape Town, he had "twisted the arms" of two Royal Navy Captains to purchase the Merino sheep the widow of a Colonel Gordan had for sale and to take them to Sydney. This is how Merino sheep came to Australia; it had nothing at all to do with John MacArthur, who received sheep from one of the Naval Captains when he had to return to England.

Elizabeth remained in England when her father died and eventually married an artist named Runciman. Mrs. King returned to Australia to live with a daughter. Eventually, all Kings lived and died in Australia, excepting Elizabeth and Gov. King.

When Mr. and Mrs. Phillip Parker King were going to England in the 170-ton ship *H.M.S. Bathurst* in which Captain P.P. King [eldest legitimate son of Gov. King born 5 February 1792] had surveyed the coast of Northern Australia, filling in the gaps left by Flinders, after leaving Cape Town and before reaching Napoleon's Prison Island of St. Helena, Henrietta King gave birth to Robert Lethbridge King on **11 February 1823**.

Mother and daughter-in-law gave birth at sea, in approximately the same place, twenty-six years apart. The dates may have been the same, for at the time the British Royal Navy had the stupid custom of changing dates at *noon*—stupid because it was different to everybody else. The Navy did alter its ways.

P.P. King, when surveying the coast around what is now Dampier, named for a swashbuckling Englishman, the first of his nation to see Australia, named some of the islands after ladies in his life. Enderby isle could be for Mr. and or Mrs. Enderby, family friends with whom he stayed when on holidays from school or the Navy. Goodwyn isle is from the maiden name of Mrs. Samuel Enderby and Mrs. Charles Enderby with whom P.P. King's sister, Anna Maria, lived most of her life, prior to becoming Mrs. Hannibal Hawkins MacArthur in 1812, Charles Enderby I being her executor until she was twenty-one. Anna's father, when Governor of Australia, sent John MacArthur, her husband's uncle, to London for Court Martial.

Hannibal's mother was a Catherine Hawkins; Charles Enderby's wife (nee Goodwyn) left a considerable portion of her estate to a Catherine Hawkins.

Since the MacArthurs came from near today's Plymouth, where the enterprising Naval Captain John Hawkins is said to have lived, although he lived in Saltash, Cornwall, on the banks of the Tamar River, it is possible the Hawkins are the same family. An isle named Gidley would be for King's grandmother, his father's mother.

Sea King Birth

Sailing home to England in a whaler was not heaven,
In seventeen hundred and ninety seven;
To avoid strife
Cmdr. P.G. King and Wife
At Cape Town changed ships
To give more room for hips
Devonshire lass Anna Coombes
Giving birth to Elizabeth avoided a watery tomb
Between the Cape and the St. Helena sanctuary
On the tenth of February.
Sailing home to England in Brig HMS Bathurst, free!
In eighteen hundred and twenty three
Capt. P.P. King's Cornish wife Henrietta
Did it better
Below the bridge
Giving birth to Robert Lethbridge
Between the Cape and the St. Helena sanctuary
On the eleventh of February.

—Keith Dawson.

THE FIRST WOMAN TO CIRCUMNAVIGATE AUSTRALIA

HMS Bathurst, a 170-ton, two-masted brig, commanded by Lt. Phillip Parker King, left Port Jackson, on 26 May 1821, with a crew of thirty-three. On 30 May, the fore-hold was opened up to reveal the thirty-fourth person, a passenger, a fourteen-year-old girl named Sarah Chambers. The previous three days had not been on a millpond. King said she was a most pitiable sight; her clothes were so filthy from four days close confinement in a dark hold, and from being dreadfully seasick, that her acquaintances, of which she had many on board, could scarcely recognise her.

Cunningham the Botanist who was onboard the *Bathurst* tells us that she had been long intimate with John Longford, the Boatswain. Mate Roe said she was a young English girl of abandoned character. *Bathurst* was going around Australia, surveying the northern and eastern coasts; King decided against turning back, so Sarah became the first female to circumnavigate Australia—not many have done it today. Sarah stated that she had come aboard without the boatswain's knowledge, but Longford had to share his rations with her. For the next 341 days, half of Longford's food, slops, bedding and tobacco were officially hers.

Cunningham said of her: "We pitied the indiscretion and folly of this young female—who could have a very inadequate idea of the barren aridity of the coast on which she would have to pass a miserable long period in a society by no means calculated to benefit the young mind and without any certain prospect of touching at any civilised port where she might introduce herself to a new society, with a view to changing her fame and fortune for the better." Cunningham noted that she joined the men with perfect content. Her privations were considerable; all ablutions went over the side. Presumably she did not fall pregnant. In the NSW census of 1828, she was listed as being of age twenty. Sarah is not mentioned again in the records.

King said of her that in a very short time, she heartily repented of her imprudence and would gladly have been re-landed, had it been possible.

Cunningham, probably, had seen more of Australia than any other person, apart from his land explorations; this was his second circumnavigation of Australia.

With acknowledgement to the book "Kings Coast" by Marsden Hordern.

EMILY CGEAGHE

In the nineteenth century, it was more likely that a female was not taught to read and write than that she was. In the early days of exploration by pack horse, keeping and carrying paper and writing materials in a readable manner was not easy and the person had to be very particular in this regard. Writing and preserving a diary in the wet tropics took extra care, so we are fortunate that this diary of an ordinary person survives.

The year was 1883, the month was May, and Mrs. Emily Caroline Cgeaghe was accompanying her husband on Ernest Faveenc's Gulf of Carpentaria expedition, starting from Normanton, Queensland, and heading west. In January, they were held up by water so that they had only reached Augusta Downs by May.

Caroline's diary, which she titled "The Little Explorers Diary," is a rarity in that it is written by a female and it has survived. The party was to the west of Leichhardt River, probably near present day Camoweal, when she noted in her diary: "**All the men amongst these blacks are circumcised.**" One wonders in horror how this operation was performed with no sharp metal instrument. Why did the aborigines do this circumcision? Health or religion or were they shown by someone? A lost tribe of Israelites? Aborigines are not known to have had sexual diseases before the arrival of Europeans, yet they were not chaste.

Prior to recording the above, Mrs. Cgeaghe states in her diary that they passed a white man's hut, which had the walls lined with aboriginal ears.

THE FIRST EUROPEAN AUSTRALIAN

Mrs. Whittle, wife of marine, drummer sergeant, Thomas Whittle, accompanied her husband on the First Fleet to Australia. On Australia Day 1788, she gave birth to a son. Unfortunately we do not know the forenames of mother or son.

Her husband and 95 other marines, together with wives and children, are not in the manifest of any of the eleven ships of the official Fleet. Were all aboard the twelfth ship, "The Ghost Ship"?

Why some Marines were allowed to bring their wives and children and others not is a mystery. Lt. Clarke of the marines wished to bring his beloved Alicia with him but was not allowed to but this sergeant and other marines were. Capt. MacArthur of the NSW Regiment was allowed to bring wife and son.

HANNA SNELL, SOLDIER

Hannah Snell (1723-92) had enlisted in 1745 as John Gray, after being deserted by her first husband, a Dutch seaman. She spent twenty-one years as a common soldier in the Army, and was not discovered by any as a woman. It was not till 1770 that she revealed her military adventures, a book of them being published under the title, *The Female Soldier: the Adventures of Hannah Snell*. One would think that alone would be sufficient for Hollywood to have made a film of her, but I suspect this is the first time you have heard of her.

She had a Pension from the Crown of £18.5.0 per annum, which is a shilling a day, and the liberty of wearing male clothing and a Cockade in her hat. She had been in barracks with seventy soldiers and not discovered by any of them, which does not say much for the British soldier of the day. Her appearance was such that she married twice after quitting the army. The forefinger of her right hand had been cut off by a sword at the taking of Pondicherry, India, which indicates she did not hang back or that she was in England all the time. Troop ships going to India did not have private cabins.

Her three marriages and the time served in the army may be due to wanderlust, as afterwards she went around the British countryside selling buttons and other small millenary from a basket on her back. I suspect that she had some form of publicity or distributing handbills as she was always to be found at a pub, the publican being the publicist in order to increase his trade.

An account of her extraordinary career will also be found in Fortescue's *History of the British Army.* Hannah was born around 1718, therefore approximately twenty-seven years old on signing up, and around forty-eight years old on receiving a pension of one shilling a day. This was sufficient for one person to live on in those days. By and large, she did better for herself than many, male or female.

Printed in the USA
CPSIA information can be obtained
at www.ICGtesting.com
LVHW091214171123
764118LV00003B/108